LISA CURRY'S
TOTAL HEALTH & FITNESS

LISA CURRY'S
TOTAL HEALTH & FITNESS

CONSULTANTS: MARGARET BARRETT, ENID GINN

Angus&Robertson
An imprint of HarperCollins*Publishers*

**Always consult your doctor before
beginning any exercise program.**

AN ANGUS & ROBERTSON BOOK
An imprint of HarperCollinsPublishers

First published in Australia in 1990
Reprinted in 1991
CollinsAngus&Robertson Publishers Pty Limited (ACN 009 913 517)
A division of HarperCollinsPublishers (Australia) Pty Limited
4 Eden Park, 31 Waterloo Road, North Ryde NSW 2113, Australia
HarperCollinsPublishers (New Zealand) Limited
31 View Road, Glenfield, Auckland 10, New Zealand
HarperCollinsPublishers Limited
77–85 Fulham Palace Road, London W6 8JB, United Kingdom

Copyright © Lisa Curry 1990

This book is copyright.
Apart from any fair dealing for the purposes of private study,
research, criticism or review, as permitted under the Copyright Act,
no part may be reproduced by any process without written
permission. Inquiries should be addressed to the publishers.

National Library of Australia
Cataloguing-in-Publication data:
Curry, Lisa, 1962–
Lisa Curry's total health & fitness.
Bibliography
ISBN 0 207 16650 1.

1. Physical fitness. 2. Exercise. I. Title. II. Title:
Health and fitness book.

Typeset in 10 pt Palatino
Printed in Australia by Griffin Press

5 4 3 2   91 92 93 94 95

To Grant, Jaimi and our newborn baby, my love,
my dreams, my happiness.

To my family for all their love and support.

To my dear coach Joe King — without him my achievements
would not have been possible.

CONTENTS

FOREWORD 3

INTRODUCTION 4

1
THE VITAL YOU 7

2
TIME MANAGEMENT 17

3
STRESS MANAGEMENT 25

4
FOOD FOR HEALTH AND FITNESS 37

5
WELL WATERED 57

6
FITNESS FROM 8 TO 80 61

7
Designing your Fitness Program **73**

    Walking **84**

    Running **92**

    Swimming **96**

    Cycling **106**

    Aerobic Dance **110**

    Weight Training **115**

    Cross Training **132**

8
Maintaining your Fitness Program ..**137**

9
Health and Sports Medicine **141**

10
There's More to Life Than Exercise ..**149**

Appendices **158**

LISA CURRY'S ACHIEVEMENTS
Started training for competition aged 11
Australian representative 1977–1990 — 23 teams/tours
Coach Joe King

MAJOR ACHIEVEMENTS

1978 Commonwealth Games, Edmonton, Canada
     World Championships, Berlin, West Germany
1980 Olympic Games, Moscow, USSR
1982 World Championships, Guayaquil, Ecuador
     Commonwealth Games Brisbane, Australia
1984 Olympic Games, Los Angeles, USA
1988 Olympic Games, Seoul, Korea (Commentator)
1989 Pan Pacific Games, Tokyo, Japan

1990 Commonwealth Games, Auckland, New Zealand
    Gold 50 m Freestyle
    Gold 100 m Butterfly
    Gold 4 x 100 m Freestyle Relay
    Gold 4 x 100 m Medley Relay
    Silver 100 m Freestyle
    <u>3 COMMONWEALTH RECORDS</u>
       50 m Freestyle 25.80
       100 m Freestyle 56.46
       100 m Butterfly 1.00.66

FOREWORD

The first time I saw Lisa Curry she looked every inch a champion. It was at the Queensland Girls G.P.S. Swimming Championships at the old Valley pool and she was only 12 years old. Shortly afterwards she walked into my swimming training quarters and I began to coach her.

The loyalty Lisa has given to her chosen sport is unwavering. Even at the tender age of 12 she sought perfection in everything she did. In a sport where most have to be pushed to train hard, she was dedicated and self-motivated. She was always ready to accomplish any training goals set her. I have used her application and subsequent successes as a motivational talking point with my squads ever since. Her outstanding comeback to international competitive swimming at the age of 27 is an example to all.

I do not know of anyone more qualified to write on the subjects contained in this book. It will be of tremendous value to those who follow the concepts and practical advice she sets out so well.

E. JOE KING
AUSTRALIAN MASTER SWIMMING COACH

INTRODUCTION

Hearing older people reminisce about 'in my time' or 'in my day' set me wondering exactly when my own time was — was I in it, had I already had it, or was I on my way to it?

At about the same time I sat down with a pile of log books I had kept since I first went to swimming training. As I flicked through the pages and read the weekly comments from my coach I began to understand why I had managed to achieve so much.

I used to spend around five hours at the pool each day, six days a week. Everything I was learning from my coach wasn't only specific to swimming, it was about everyday life — how to get the most out of life, how to feel good about myself and imagine myself being successful, how to recognise opportunities and take them.

Looking back, everything seems to have worked out perfectly, but it wasn't all roses. I had my doubts, cried, put on weight, felt ugly, depressed and lonely. But understanding why I was feeling like this and working out ways to deal with it enabled me to pull through.

Everyone can learn skills to overcome these inevitable negative feelings. You must believe in yourself, have the courage to do whatever you want, be honest with yourself and aim for your goals with determination, enthusiasm and persistence. Try and strive for excellence, take every opportunity that presents itself and be responsible for yourself.

If you look around, you will see people who are in all sorts of shape — some good, some not so good, some pretty bad. Most people at some stage desire to change something about themselves. Although many books, magazines and videos tell women that thin is fashionable, they neglect the fact that thin means nothing if you're not healthy to go with it.

Slim doesn't mean healthy.
Fat doesn't mean healthy.
Fit means healthy.

The aim of this book is to encourage you to strive not simply for thinness, but for fitness and health. A fit person has an abundance of energy and vitality, glowing good looks and high self-confidence. There are many factors that make up such a balanced high-energy lifestyle. You need a positive mental attitude, be able to use your time efficiently and have time for yourself, rest and relaxation. You need to control stress, have a well-planned consistent exercise program and a balanced nutritional diet. Learn to manage your emotions, feel worthwhile and loved, and enjoy good restful sleep.

I don't expect you to eat like a rabbit or train like an Olympian (unless of course you want to be an Olympian). The advice that follows can be used and adapted to your everyday life, starting from today. Radical changes will not happen overnight, but you will be pleasantly surprised just how easy it is to feel energised, vital and confident. You will soon discover the rewards of a happy and healthy lifestyle.

If you are one of those people who often say 'if only' or 'I wish' then by the end of this book you may find yourself saying 'Why didn't I do that earlier?'.

I have decided that my time is now and that I should look after this body of mine. After all, I have to live in it for the rest of my life. Your time is also now. Time for you to get fit and healthy.

CONSULTANTS

MARGARET BARRETT

Margaret is a Queenslander who has a keen interest in nutrition and sports medicine. She has a healthy lifestyle and a university degree in Human Movement Studies. She is proficient in many sports that require her to be at peak fitness including the triathlon, marathon, stair climbing, mountain racing and surf-lifesaving. She has competed at numerous international events in her chosen sports.

ENID GINN

Enid is the Coaching Development and Sports Research Liaison Officer at the University of Queensland and is currently completing a PhD in exercise physiology. She has played representative hockey for Queensland at senior and veteran level and coached the sport for many years. She has developed fitness programs for hockey players as well as the 1988 Olympic diving and kayaking teams. Her numerous other sporting interests include sailing, softball, squash, athletics, swimming, snow skiing, sailboarding, surfing, table tennis and golf.

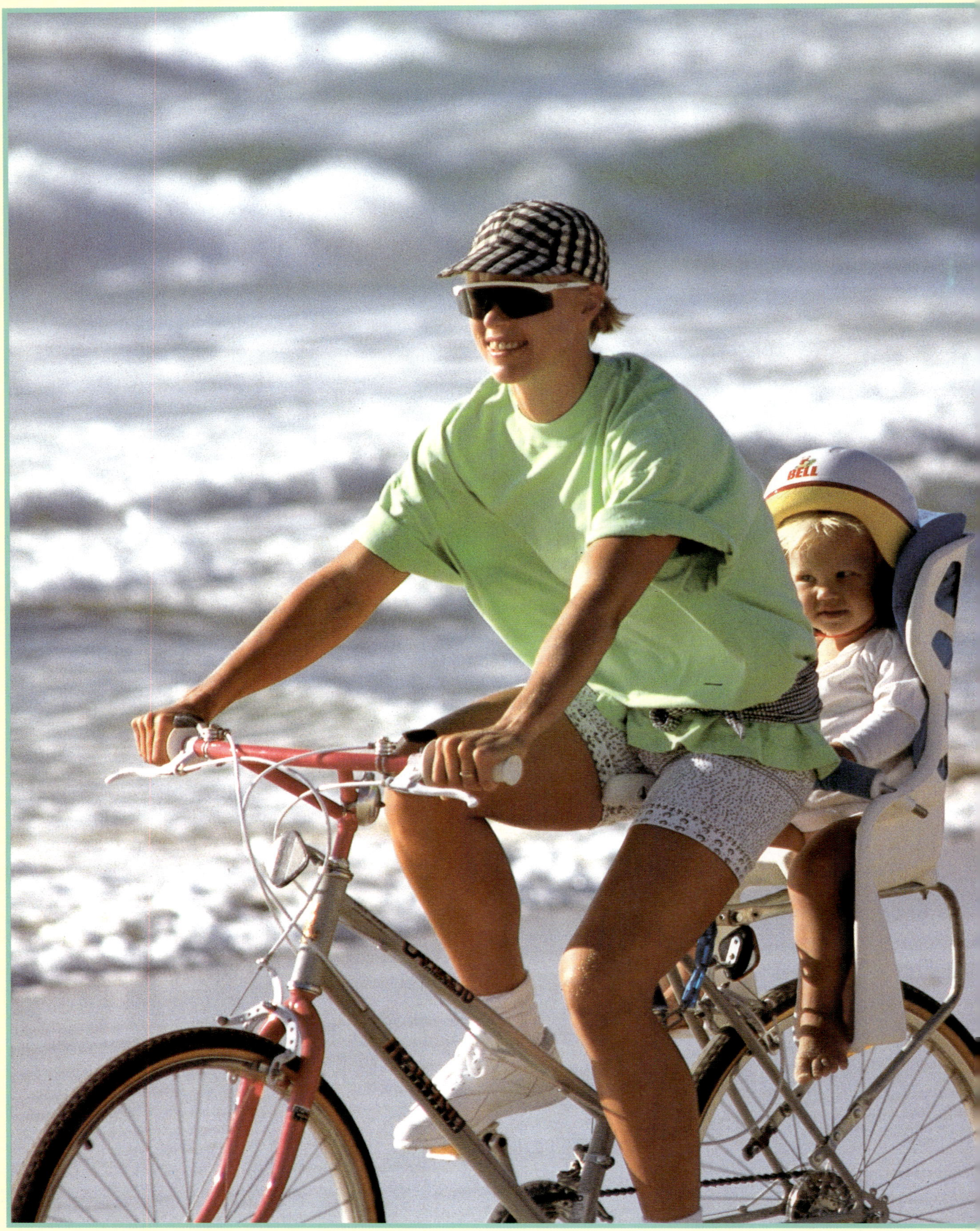
BELL

CHAPTER ONE

THE VITAL YOU

ARE YOU HAPPY WITH EVERYTHING ABOUT YOURSELF?

Are you satisfied with your physical appearance, health, fitness level, outlook on life, emotions, relationships, family and work? If you could choose to be anyone in the world, you should choose to be yourself. Such a choice comes from living a high-energy balanced lifestyle where your vitality is at its peak. Vitality is something that seems to exude from some people. It is hard to put your finger on why. They always seem to have more energy and zest for living. What's their secret?

There is no secret. Vitality is not magical, it comes from confronting your whole person and striving to enrich it. Vitality comes from being in control of your body, your environment, your work, your relaxation, your mental outlook, your relationships and above all, being responsible for yourself. Vital people don't settle for anything less than their best. When you are not sick, are you happy just considering yourself well? Vital people aren't. They expect and aim for more than being well. In fact they don't even expect to get sick. They aspire to function physically, mentally and emotionally at peak level.

Secretly some people believe they can never be at that peak level — feeling, looking and being great. Their self doubts come from the fear of what they will have to do without, what they will have to make time for, and what they will have to put up with to get where they want to be.

The following will explore what vitality means for you and how to achieve it without those fears. Taken step by step and day by day it's easily manageable and definitely worth the effort.

YOUR BODY

First impressions are formed simply by the way you look. Whether you like it or not this can affect many areas of your life — career, romance, opportunities. A person who cares about their appearance shows part of their personality.

You constantly carry a mental image of your physical appearance wherever you go. It is reflected in your confidence and assertiveness. Many women, for example, believe that the more beautiful they are, the better the impression they will make. But the age old saying that beauty is in the eye of the beholder is true. We all have some feature that makes us beautiful; it may be your eyes, your hair, or your smile.

The way others see you and the way you see yourself is important. So is looking after your body, inside as well as outside. A beautiful smile is ruined by decayed teeth; hair looks drab if it has lost its lustre and sheen. A wholesome balanced diet with regular exercise is an easy way to natural good looks. Your total appearance is enhanced by careful attention to skin care, hairstyle and make-up. Concentrate on your individuality and experiment with different styles.

Smoking, alcohol and drugs are detrimental to your body. Statistics show that the habit of smoking is unfortunately becoming increasingly popular with women as a means of weight control and relaxation. Not only does smoking harm the body internally, it also affects your breath and your skin. Make the right choices about your body. You are unique and deserve the best.

THE ENVIRONMENT

The physical environment plays an important part in your well-being. Do you like what you see when you look out the window? The place where you spend most of your time should be as pleasant as possible. Improve your surroundings to give yourself a boost each day. Plant a tree, pot a plant or arrange some special things in your home or office.

Try and avoid living in a constantly noisy environment. It can be particularly stressful as it affects your concentration, ability to sleep and your peace of mind. Similarly, an environment that is too crowded can wear you down. Having personal space is most important.

The sun, wind, cold and pollution are harsh environmental factors that need to be controlled. A sun tan is considered a sign of beauty, health and vitality and every summer thousands of people lie unprotected on our beaches in pursuit of the golden tan. But tanning is a major cause of premature ageing, and can often lead to skin cancer. Protect yourself from the sun by using a sunscreen suited to your skin type. In the Australian sun a full protection cream is

THE VITAL YOU

essential as well as a hat. The colour of your face can always be made darker with make-up if required. This way your skin will keep its youthfulness and vitality for a lot longer.

Added to the dangers of over-exposure from ultraviolet rays is the heat given off by the sun. Heat is a stress in itself, and exercising in the heat is potentially dangerous unless precautions are taken. Try to avoid over-exertion in the hottest part of the day. If you do exercise, tone down your intensity level as the body is already expending more energy just keeping itself cool. It is important to always drink water before and at regular intervals during exercise. If you know you will be exercising in hot weather, take care to drink a lot of water the day before. Hydrating the system two hours in advance is a trick often used by elite endurance athletes.

As well as our own bodies, a foetus is particularly susceptible to the effects of heat. Women in the first trimester of pregnancy should therefore avoid exercising during the hottest part of the day, taking saunas or wearing 'plastics' to make them sweat.

Refreshing and invigorating, water is also necessary for good health.

Flotation tanks are becoming increasingly popular as a means of relaxation.

Learn to use the environment in a positive way. Water has many other benefits. It is a natural cleanser and an essential part of our health. Water is great for your skin and enables your kidneys to operate more efficiently. It also keeps your whole system in better order. It is, however, possible to shower too frequently as this removes natural oils that act as moisturisers for your body.

You cannot drink too much water. In fact, most people don't drink enough. Approximately 60 per cent of our body is composed of water. Once you feel thirsty your body is already below its required amount. Get into the habit of drinking water regularly. Keep a water bottle on your desk at work. At home, keep a cold jug of water in the fridge rather than soft drink or cordial. You should aim to drink enough so you rarely feel thirsty.

Water is also a wonderful medium for relaxation. Just listening to water running or the sound of the sea can calm your mind. Flotation tanks are a popular device for relaxation and meditation. You simply float in an enclosed tank of water. Some believe that this comforting state simulates our foetal stage when we were surrounded by water.

WORK AND RELAXATION

We all spend a certain amount of our day working, whether it is in the outside workforce, or in the home with children. The rest of the day should be ours for relaxation, recreation and sleep.

Achieving a balance between work and relaxation is essential to good health and vitality. In today's world success is often measured by dollars and status. Many people strive for the highest levels in these areas and are left with no time or energy to have fun.

When it is time for recreation you can still be productive. Take up an interest that inspires some self-improvement. This can be a sport, something creative or perhaps cultural. Time spent in this way is not wasted time. The accumulation of work-related stress starts to take its toll only after we have ignored the need for relaxation. Picture in your mind an overworked, overstressed person. This image is not one of health, beauty or vitality. The key to achieving and benefiting from a balance between work and relaxation is time management.

MENTAL OUTLOOK

The potential of the mind is virtually unknown. We only use a small percentage of our brain power. What we do know, however, is that well-being of the mind is a vital element of health.

We are all continually learning new things. The process doesn't stop when we leave school. Every new experience influences our direction and perception of ourselves and others. Learning is food for the mind; the more we know, the more we appreciate our world and ourselves. Often something we fear in life is simply something we know nothing about. Be willing to listen, enquire and learn from others.

Try to be enthusiastic in whatever you do. If it's your work, accept that no job is always enjoyable — otherwise we'd all be doing it. Look for the rewarding aspects and concentrate on them.

How you really feel about yourself, your self-esteem, is very important. Our sense of self identity is formulated in our teenage years. As adults there are always some things we'd like to change. If someone promised to change these things for us or said that we didn't have to accept them, we'd all jump at the chance. But privately we may remain unconvinced whether this could really be possible.

Developing the practice of positive thinking and taking action to accomplish something enhances your self-esteem. Believe in yourself and build a positive

LISA CURRY'S TOTAL HEALTH & FITNESS

self-image. Remind yourself daily that you are a worthwhile person and deserve the best. A person's level of self-confidence and self-esteem is a major contributor to their vitality. But recognise that this level can vary at different stages throughout your life.

Our feelings or emotions also control our mental outlook. In the space of one day we can experience many different feelings including happiness, sadness, anger, frustration, boredom, love, excitement, anticipation and so on.

It is not necessarily bad to experience negative feelings. If a close friend moves away it is natural to feel sad. Expression of our feelings is an important part of health and well-being. It is more socially acceptable for women to express their emotions, but this has created a myth that women are 'more emotional', which of course is not true. Unfortunately men are taught from their formative years that if they show what they feel they are not being 'a man'. This conditioning can have disastrous results if pent-up feelings do not find a suitable outlet.

When negative feelings do occur it is important to feel and acknowledge them, but not to dwell on them. Recognise their cause and understand that all feelings are only temporary and will pass. Don't become frustrated if you can't seem to shake yourself out of bad feelings. Take positive steps — talk to a friend, set yourself a rewarding task and keep occupied. Remember to take one day at a time. As they say — today is the first day of the rest of your life.

When positive feelings occur — happiness, excitement, love — revel in them. Laugh often and laugh out loud. Laughter lines and sparkling eyes are naturally beautiful. Sit back and laugh at yourself; it is a marvellous remedy for feeling blue.

> 'Successful people are not afraid to fail. They have the ability to accept their failures and continue on, knowing that failure is a natural consequence of trying. The law of failure is one of the most powerful of all the success laws because you only really fail when you quit trying.'

Control of your mind plays an important part in developing willpower. Willpower is not something someone else can do for you. It is often needed when we are feeling bored or anxious and we are alone with the fridge. How can you learn to say no to yourself? Recognise situations where you know you will be tempted. Make a written list to help you avoid them in future. If the situation simply cannot be avoided, don't try and pretend it's not happening. Confront it. One voice tells you how nice it would be while another tries desperately hard to remind you of the long-term consequences. If you fail, don't worry. The odd occasion that gets right out of hand makes us stop and think. Recognise your mood when your willpower was low. When we're bored many of us look for something to eat. Be prepared when boredom begins and have a plan. It can be something as simple as walking twice around the house, or perhaps taking yourself to an aerobics class. When you activate the plan the boredom will disappear. Find out what works best for you.

Adopt the right attitude to help your willpower. Instead of thinking 'here I go again, I knew this would happen, I won't be able to stop', try to adopt a positive attitude. Say to yourself 'here is one of those awful situations, I've recognised it and identified how I feel, I'm halfway there'. Then work out what action you can take to remain in control. Never underestimate how strong your mind is and how much you can create change by the way you think. It's simply a matter of taking the right steps.

RELATIONSHIPS

Human beings are social beings. Our relationship with others is an important contribution to our quality of life. Some people seem lonely, bitter, unsociable or withdrawn and have very few friends. Good relationships mean warmth, happiness, trust and support — all essential ingredients for well-being.

Think about the different people in your life who are close to you and important to you. They are probably your family, your partner and a few close friends. Why are these particular people so important? Usually it is because we can be completely ourselves with them. They can see us at our worst — when we've burnt the dinner, lost our wallet, with a pimple, or in an old dressing gown — and they still treat us and love us just the same. They don't expect us to be anything other than what we are, nor we them.

Our partner is the person we choose to share our life

with on a day to day basis, the other half of our team. Perhaps we are all not at this stage in our lives right now, but it is an experience nearly all of us will have at some time. This special relationship must be cultivated. It's easy to put time into other things — a work project, recreation, and friends — and take that one person for granted. Arrange special time to have alone with your partner, without the children and without others. Sometimes you will both be so busy with work and family that you may need to make appointments with each other. Making time to develop good relationships with others is important to our health and vitality.

SELF RESPONSIBILITY

You are responsible for yourself. While this appears to be stating the obvious, many of us give the responsibility of ourselves to someone else. It may seem easier at the time, but living this way guarantees we will fall short of our full potential.

When we are having trouble making a decision, we often look to a significant person in our lives to make the decision for us. They proceed to tell us what is best for us, what we need and what we think. Such a process erodes a small part of our self identity. It also gives us the chance to blame someone else if we make the wrong choice.

Blaming someone or something else is a popular escape. It saves you from the fear of failure or of making a mistake. Some people go to incredible lengths to avoid making mistakes. If you make your own choices and face the consequences, you can experience one of life's valuable lessons. All great people have made mistakes. Successful people use their mistakes, learn by them and take action not to repeat them. If you never risk failing, you will never take any risk at all. You may not know failure, but you will also never know success. Working through personal failure develops strength of character and a knowledge that you can cope. This provides a vital base for self-esteem and self-confidence.

No one else can really ever be responsible for your actions or feelings. If we believe they can, we lose control of ourselves. Our base of self worth becomes dependent on someone else's responses rather than our own. If they stopped liking us, we would be in danger of no longer liking ourselves. Remember you are not here always to please someone else. This may sound selfish, but you must be aware of and look after your own needs. If your needs are not met, you cannot grow as a whole person.

★ ★ ★

There are no limits to the boundaries of exploring change in all these things, only the limits you put on yourself. These areas will be examined more fully and the methods for achieving positive health in all aspects of your life will be further outlined. It's a complex business, but by confronting each area at a time, step by step, you will enrich your life.

We are about to break some old habits and replace them with some new ones. By working towards clear goals you will increase the quality of your life a great deal. The repercussions are enormous.

> 'Going far beyond the call of duty, doing more than others expect... this is what excellence is all about. And it comes from striving, maintaining the highest standards, looking after the smallest detail, and going the extra mile. Excellence means doing your very best, in everything, in every way.'

Have a positive attitude and pursue what you want out of life, though this should not interfere with what other people want out of their lives.

Self-discipline is the key to personal freedom. It helps us use our time to the best advantage.

You can be your biggest time waster! Realise your needs and priorities and attend to them.

Chasing after time is bad for your health. Learning to say 'no' is a necessary skill for anyone whose time is valuable.

CHAPTER TWO

TIME MANAGEMENT

THERE NEVER SEEMS TO BE ENOUGH TIME FOR EVERYTHING WE'D LIKE TO DO

Many people often use the excuse that they can't find the time to exercise. To constantly chase after time is detrimental to your health. Instead of trying to save time we should learn to manage it.

The first step is to find out how you spend your time each day. Rule up a pad with three columns as shown below.

For two consecutive days keep a diary of every activity you do during the day.

TIME	ACTIVITY	CRITICAL COMMENTS

Choose fairly typical days (not the weekend) when you are following your normal routines. Carry the pad with you and jot down the type of activity, the approximate time taken and any comments that occur to you. You will need to make entries at frequent intervals during the day. Obviously keeping the diary will also take up some of your time.

At the end of the two days add up the time taken for each activity. Treat the two days separately. Work out what percentage of your time each activity took up, for example, if you slept for 8 hours it would be 33% of the 24 hours. Look at the similarities and differences between your two days. On your pad number off each activity in order of importance. This should include the importance of leisure and relaxation time, not just work matters. Assess how much of your time was used on areas that are relatively unimportant to you. Take note of how much of your day was taken up by interruptions and trivial time wasting.

Once you have discovered where your time goes, ask yourself which are the most dissatisfying areas of the list and what you can do to change them.

Grant makes the most of his time by taking Jaimi Lee for a 'running' walk.

PRIORITIES

A good manager of time is someone who can order in priority all the facets of their life. Working out your priorities simply means choosing to do one thing first rather than something else. However, if this is an unconscious choice, the decisions are not always made in accordance with clear objectives.

Bad habits can influence the choice. For example, it is easier to approach trivial things and finish them before we tackle the more important, complex matters. We do things that are planned, have deadlines or have the resources immediately available before other things. We do things for those we see as important people first. Women often consider the needs of others, particularly the family, before themselves.

All these habits pattern the course of our time. Instead we need to make clear choices about what is important to us. There are five aspects of life which most people consider a priority — career, family, friends, leisure and self-development. We should ensure that we allocate time to each of them.

TIME MANAGEMENT

A DAILY AND WEEKLY PLAN

An effective way to control what we do with our time is to plan it in advance. We usually make a mental note of things we want to get done, but often these don't eventuate. Get into the habit of formulating a written weekly and daily plan. A weekly plan should be a list of all the activities you would like to accomplish within the week. Don't forget to include all aspects of your life.

The daily plan should have time schedules for allocating activities to be worked on that day. Major tasks in your weekly plan — for example, spring cleaning or a research project — can be broken up into sizeable chunks. This way they become much less threatening. You are more likely to complete a project that not only has a beginning, but also has a clearly defined end.

ASSERTIVENESS

What does assertiveness have to do with time management? Learning to say 'no' is a necessary skill for anyone whose time is valuable. This is called being assertive. It comes from having a positive attitude to yourself and knowing it is alright to pursue what you want out of life. In return you must also recognise that you should not interfere with what other people want out of their life.

How can you be assertive if a person interrupts you with something they consider important, but you don't, especially when you haven't time for it in your daily plan? There are three different responses in any given situation:

1 Non-assertive — when you give in.
2 Aggressive — when you win at all costs.
3 Assertive — when you stand up for your rights without interfering with the rights of others.

GOALS

It can be difficult sorting out priorities if our goals are undefined. The most successful people in the world have their goals in priority. A simple exercise is to write down on a sheet of paper 15 things you'd love to accomplish in your life. Pretend there are no obstacles and let your imagination wander. Now write a number beside each in order of priority with (1) as the goal you desire most. Although some of your goals may be beyond the realms of possibility, take each in turn and write next to it five things you would need to have accomplished within the next year for this goal to be a tiny bit closer to you. Keep your list tucked inside this book and see if you are making any progress next time you consult it.

The following situation illustrates the three different responses: after you finish work you have planned to buy something for dinner, pay the Bankcard bill and get petrol before picking up your daughter from preschool. A friend has car trouble and asks if you would mind giving her a lift home. This is out of your way and would prevent you completing any of your tasks.

These are three possible responses to her:

1 Non-assertive. 'Well, er . . . I've got a few things to do after work. I suppose I could put them off, but I'll have to pick up my daughter on the way.'
2 Aggressive. 'I've got a million and one things to do this afternoon and couldn't possibly find an extra second. That car of your needs more regular services.'
3 Assertive. 'I've a number of jobs this afternoon which I'm aiming to get done before I pick up my daughter. Perhaps you could help me with these. Alternatively I would be happy to drop you on my way at a convenient bus stop or train station.'

Being assertive is not being rude. It is simply realising your needs and priorities and attending to them. This way you are not threatened by other people's different needs, nor do you feel obliged to change or devalue your own. If you express yourself honestly and directly, you will experience an overall sense of well-being and self-respect. Your relationships with others will feel more comfortable and be more rewarding. Differences between people will no longer be perceived as threatening.

Your non-verbal or body language must also echo your assertiveness. Your gestures and posture must be consistent with what you are saying. You should always maintain firm eye contact with the person to whom you are speaking. The assertive person is more in control of themselves and their time.

YOU — YOUR OWN WORST ENEMY

While other people can create major interruptions to your time, there is an even bigger time waster — yourself. Here are a few suggestions for eliminating wasted time in some common areas.

Paperwork Whether we're employed in the outside workforce or responsible for the household accounts (or both), most of us have a constant pile of paperwork and reading matter on our desks that builds faster than it ever decreases. Each time you pick up a piece of paper get into the habit of deciding its importance. Should you take action on it immediately, does it need to be carefully absorbed or can it be thrown away. The extra few seconds taken to make this decision can save hours.

Travel While travel itself isn't wasted time, what we do with our time when we travel often is. Whether you are a passenger flying, travelling by public transport or driving your own car, travel is an excellent opportunity to utilise time. If you're not driving take along some reading matter, write a letter or set out your daily or weekly plan. If you have a cassette player in your car buy or tape talks concerning your area of interest and listen to them while you drive.

START THE DAY RIGHT

Some form of vigorous early morning activity can give you a great start to the day. Set aside enough time to spend 30 minutes minimum getting your body moving — go for a walk, a run, or hop on a stationary bike. Each activity will get you fit and help burn extra kilojoules.

Start your day with a full body stretch. Drink a couple of glasses of cool water. Allow time for a good healthy breakfast. This will prevent you from experiencing that mid-morning tiredness. Make a positive affirmation and run through your daily plan.

Listen to a self-motivation tape. If you have difficulty finding the time to exercise park a little further from your destination and take your walking shoes with you. Get off your bus or train a few stops earlier and briskly walk home or to work. Of course, depending on your mood, travelling can also be a good time to relax by reading or listening to music.

Communication A great deal of our time is wasted through bad communication. Often we are not exactly sure what it is we are saying. This, combined with the fact that most people usually only half listen, makes us slow communicators. The key to effective communication is to keep it clear and simple.

Procrastination This is a common human fault that costs money in business and hours of our personal time. It is a bad habit that we need to recognise and remedy. When you hear yourself saying 'I must do that sometime', stop yourself and do it immediately. Setting long- and short-term goals is another way of becoming more efficient and beating procrastination, 'the thief of time'.

Personal Organisation

It takes tremendous effort to beat disorganisation in our lives. Disorganisation is an ingrained habit that prevents us from achieving our plan for the day. It is no use planning to accomplish something before work if it takes us 30 minutes to find our car keys. Identify the small things that delay your time. Attack each little slip you make and aim to behave differently. Plan ahead. For example, have your clothes ready for the next day, keep your car's petrol tank half full, and get up when your alarm goes off. Don't sway from your determination to be better organised until your new and better habits are firmly embedded. Soon this newly learned behaviour will become automatic.

Self-discipline

Many of us fight the idea of self-discipline. We associate it with being a child and having discipline forced upon us. But self-discipline is actually the key to personal freedom. It is a positive attitude that helps us use our time to the best advantage. Think about the words in the first column. A self-disciplined approach has been added in the second column.

soon	now
when	today
I wish	I will
perhaps	it's happening
nearly there	success
if only	on time

By examining our thought processes and changing them we can save ourselves time in achieving our goals.

The truth is that we will never have the time to achieve everything we want to, however good our intentions. There will always be something that needs doing. But by sorting out your priorities, making a daily and weekly plan, being assertive and taking steps to eliminate wasted time you could save yourself more than two hours every day. Consider this: to increase your fitness level and control your weight takes no more than 30 minutes a day.

Time Management

'The purpose of goals is to focus our attention. The mind will not reach toward achievement until it has clear objectives. The magic begins when we set goals. It is then that the switch is turned on, the current begins to flow, and the power to accomplish becomes a reality.'

'Each problem has hidden in it an opportunity so powerful that it literally dwarfs the problem. The greatest success stories were created by people who recognised a problem and turned it into an opportunity.'

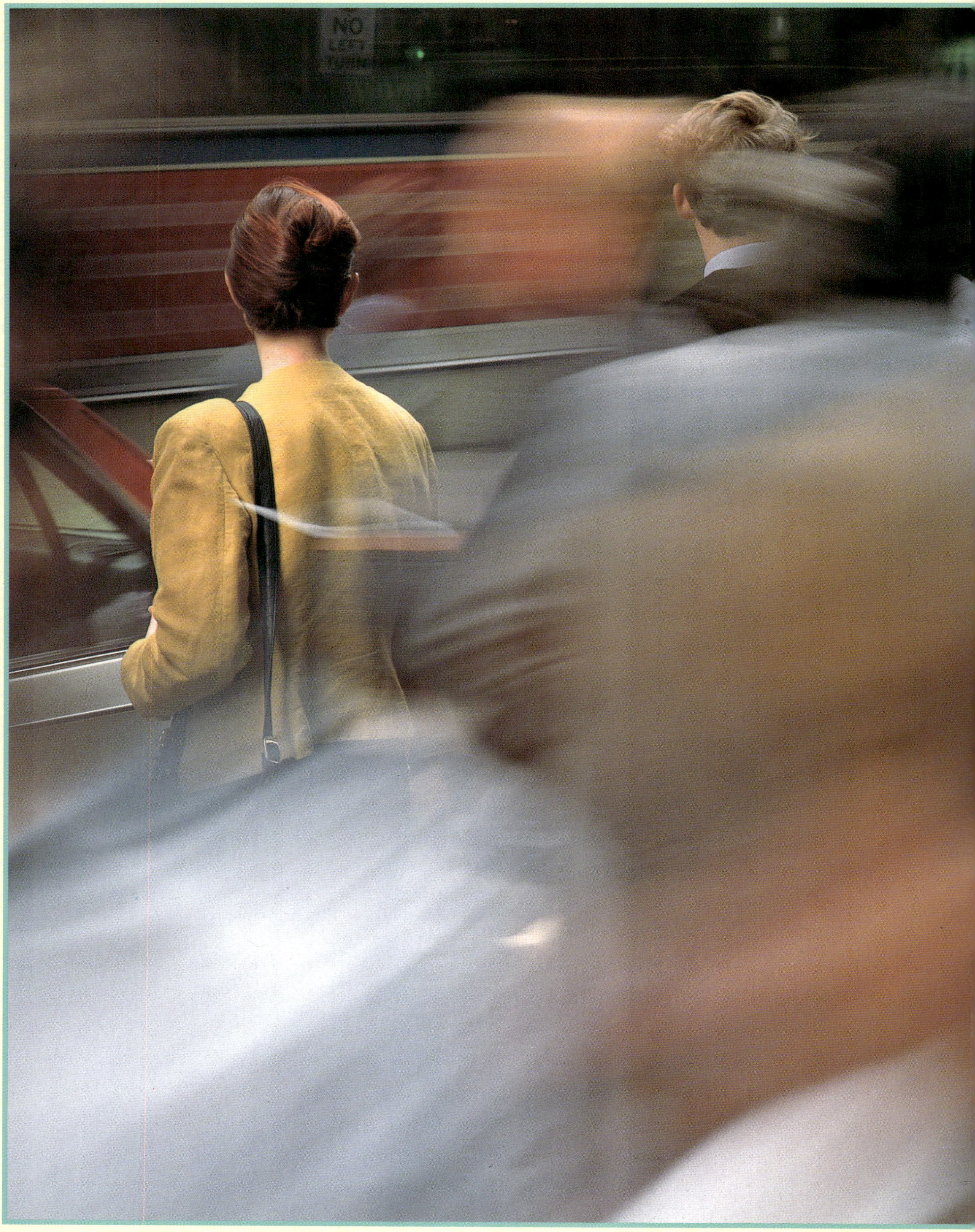
NO

CHAPTER THREE

STRESS MANAGEMENT

STRESS IS AN INEVITABLE BUT CONTROLLABLE PART OF LIFE

The phenomenon of stress has been widely publicised lately. There have been many dire warnings about the ill effects of stress, but stress is an inevitable part of life.

WHAT EXACTLY IS STRESS?

Stress is the applied force or pressure exerted on one thing by another. In physics putting too much stress on something causes it to break. But if no stress is applied, things never move or change, so a certain amount of stress can be very healthy. You can see how this principle relates to humans.

The 'Kamin Curve' represents the effect of stress levels on your performance.

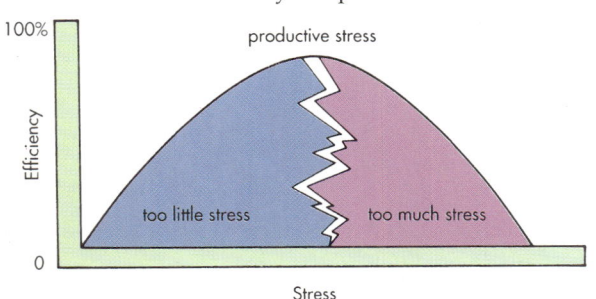

WORK STRETCH

Take a break from the computer, desk, meeting — whatever requires you to sit for a period of time. Give your body a boost with a quick whole body stretch. Hold for 30 seconds. Repeat. Deep belly breathe for 30 seconds. Repeat when feeling tired.

At a low level of stress, such as in an unchallenging and repetitive job, motivation and consequently performance are low. The person may feel that their life is in a rut. This could typically manifest itself in various changes of behaviour, for example, eating or drinking in excess.

As you can see from the curve, the same behaviour changes and high levels of anxiety or tension are experienced by the person who is under a great deal of stress. The level of performance drops once the stress level is elevated.

The ideal is to achieve a balance and control your stress level. This way your performance is at its peak and you experience a true sense of well-being.

People who continue under high levels of stress for long periods of time literally get worn down, and sooner or later their physical and emotional health are affected. The effects of stress vary greatly from one person to another. They can include relatively minor effects such as irritability, overeating, migraine or heartburn to serious diseases. All these effects occur when the stress is no longer positive.

What actually happens to your body when it is placed under stress? The body's general reactions to stress are the same for

STRESS MANAGEMENT

everyone. When a stressful stimulus is exerted on a human their body automatically switches to a mode that enables it to be fully prepared to either defend itself or flee from the situation. This response is an inbuilt lifesaving device and is called the fight or flight response.

★ ★ ★

As shown in the diagram, a full and definite process takes place within the body under stress. Priority areas are the muscles, to make the body ready for physical action, and the heart, so that it can pump more blood to the muscles. The lungs also need to provide more oxygen to the muscles for energy and to the brain for it to be more alert. High-energy foods such as sugars and fats are released into the blood. At the same time the flow of oxygen to the digestive system is cut off to provide as much blood as possible to the muscles. This is why, at these moments of crisis, you never have an appetite.

When the crisis is over all these aspects are reversed. When the crisis becomes a long-term persistent stress, the body remains in a chronic state of fight or flight. The result is high blood pressure, digestive problems, muscular pain and possible

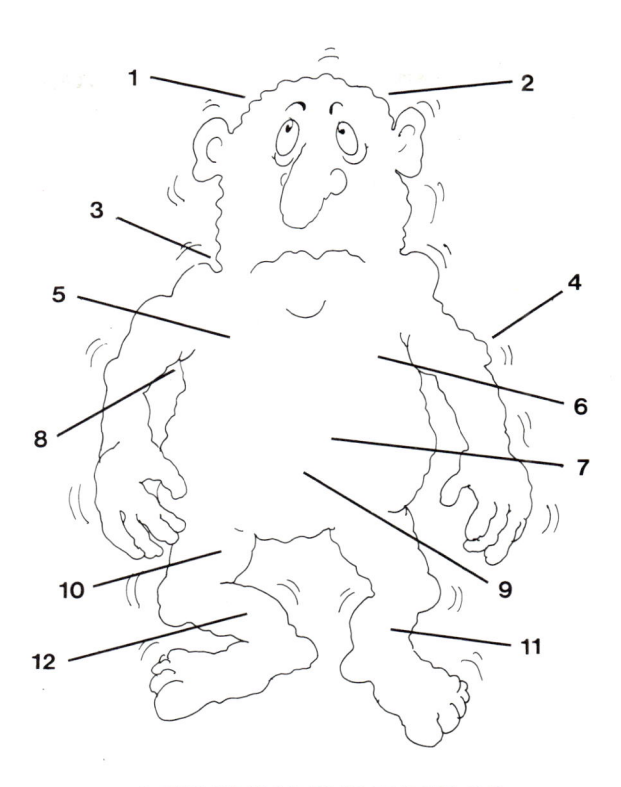

ACTIVATING THE FIGHT OR FLIGHT RESPONSE

1. The brain receives the stimulus of danger from eyes, ears, etc.
2. The brain activates:
   (a) the pituitary gland to release hormones
   (b) the involuntary nervous system to send signals via nerves to various parts of the body.
3. 2(a) and 2(b) cause the adrenal glands to release the hormones adrenalin, non-adrenalin and cortisones. These lead to all the other changes described here:
4. Mentally alert — senses activated.
5. Breathing rate speeds up — nostrils and air passages in lungs open wider to get air in more quickly.
6. Heartbeat speeds up and blood pressure rises.
7. Liver releases sugar, cholesterol and fatty acids into the blood to supply quick energy to the muscles.
8. Sweating increases to help cool the body.
9. Blood clotting ability increases, preparing for possible injury.
10. Muscles of the bladder and bowel openings contract and non-lifesaving activity of body ceases temporarily.
11. Blood is diverted to the muscles and muscle fibres tense, ready for action.
12. Immunity responses decrease — useful in short term to allow massive response by body — but harmful over a long period.

disease. It all makes sense when you relate this back to the actual state the body is in. Diseases of the modern world, such as cancer and heart disease, have been found to have a definite correlation to stress.

Learning how to recognise, reorganise and control your stress is not only beneficial to your well-being and performance, it can be a matter of life or death.

ARE YOU STRESSED?

Stress is an accumulative thing. It can sometimes seem to take only one small thing to make you snap, when actually there have been a number of other factors already operating.

Here are three separate tests to help you determine whether or not you are functioning under too much stress. The combination of results should give you a good indication of how stressed you are at the moment.

AUTOMATIC THOUGHTS QUESTIONNAIRE

One of the factors that can affect your ability to deal with stress is your own thought patterns. Using the scale:

1 = not at all   2 = sometimes   3 = moderately often   4 = often   5 = all the time

rate your responses to the following 20 statements:

Today things just aren't going my way . . . . . . ____
I can't seem to pull myself together . . . . ____
It is so difficult to succeed . . . . ____
People often don't understand me . . . . ____
At times I'm weak . . . . ____
I feel totally disorganised . . . . ____
I can't get started . . . . ____
My life is not going well . . . . ____
I've let people down . . . . ____
What is wrong with me today? . . . . ____
The future doesn't look good . . . . ____

I don't know how I'm going to get
   everything done . . . . ____
I'm disappointed in myself . . . . ____
I certainly got out of the wrong side of
   the bed today . . . . ____
I'm not looking forward to tomorrow . . . . . . ____
Things can only get better . . . . ____
I can do better than this . . . . ____
There's not enough time to get everything
   done . . . . ____
I'm just not keeping up . . . . ____
This week has been very stressful . . . . ____

Now add up your total. There is no excellent score. You simply repeat this test again in two weeks, aiming to decrease the result.

LIFE EVENTS

The 'Holmes-Rahe Survey of Recent Experiences' is a scale of life events, which are each allocated a score. This score will tell you what level of stress you are dealing with at the moment. However, it will not tell you how much stress you are actually experiencing, this depends more on your coping skills.

This test is used as a predictor of your future health and you should aim to repeat it annually. Add up your total points from the following list of events that you have experienced in your life in the last 12 months:

LIFE EVENTS	SCORE	LIFE EVENTS	SCORE
death of partner	100	son or daughter leaving home	29
divorce	73	trouble with in-laws	29
separation	65	outstanding personal achievement	28
gaol term	63	partner begins or stops work	26
death of close family member	63	begin or finish school	26
personal injury or illness	53	change in living conditions	25
marriage	50	revision of personal habits	24
fired at work	47	trouble with boss	23
reconciliation with partner	45	change in residence	20
retirement	45	change in work hours or activities	20
change in health of family member	44	change in schools	20
business readjustment	40	change in church activities	19
pregnancy	39	change in social activities	18
sexual difficulties	39	mortgage or loan less than $60 000	17
change of financial state	38	change in sleeping habits	16
death of close friend	37	change in number of family get togethers	15
change to a different line of work	36	change in eating habits	15
change in number of arguments with partner	35	vacation	13
mortgage of more than $60 000	31	Christmas	12
foreclosure of mortgage or loan	30	minor violation of the law	11
change in responsibilities at work	29	**TOTAL**	

More than 300 you are quite likely to be seriously ill in the near future.

Between 200–300 you could experience some serious health problems.

Less than 200 you are much less likely to be seriously ill in the future.

LIFESTYLE ASSESSMENT

This test, the 'Miller-Smith Lifestyle Assessment Inventory', aims to determine the amount of stress resulting from your lifestyle. There are no right or wrong answers, but the more honest you are the more useful the test is.

Rate your answers to the 20 statements according to the following scale:

1 = almost always   2 = often   3 = sometimes   4 = occasionally   5 = almost never

I get at least one hot, balanced meal a day . . . _____
I get 7 to 8 hours sleep at least 4 nights a week . . . . _____
I give and receive affection regularly . . . . . . _____
I have at least one relative within 50 kilometres on whom I can rely . . . . _____
I exercise to the point of perspiration at least twice a week . . . . _____
I smoke less than half a packet of cigarettes a day (non-smokers score 1) . . . . _____
I take fewer than 5 alcoholic drinks a week . . . . _____
I am the appropriate weight for my height . . . _____
I have an income adequate to meet basic expenses . . . . _____
I get strength from my religious beliefs or I feel comfortable with my view of the universe and my place in it . . . . _____

I regularly attend club or social activities . . . . _____
I have a network of friends and acquaintances . . . . _____
I have one or more friends to confide in about personal matters . . . . _____
I am in good health (including eyesight, hearing, teeth) . . . . _____
I am able to speak openly about my feelings when angry or worried . . . . _____
I have regular conversations with the people I live with about domestic problems or chores and money . . . . _____
I do something for fun at least once a week . . . . _____
I am able to organise my time effectively . . . . _____
I drink fewer than 3 cups of coffee a day . . . . _____
I take quiet time for myself during the day . . . . _____

Add up your total. From this you can obtain some general indication of how much your lifestyle is making you prone to stress according to the results:

Score	Indicates
under 50	= low vulnerability
50–70	= vulnerable to stress
70–95	= seriously vulnerable
more than 95	= extremely vulnerable

The results from these three self tests should give you a good overall indication of how much stress has accumulated in your life. Understanding and being aware of these factors are most important when learning to control your own stress levels. The scores are not something that you can compare with someone else. Each individual is very different. Repeat the Automatic Thoughts Questionnaire and the Lifestyle Assessment tests again in two weeks and notice any changes in your result. By the end of this chapter you should have some new ideas and techniques to help you control your stress more effectively.

STRESS CONTROL

Medication A common remedy recommended to people to deal with their stress is to take some sort of medication. Every week medical practitioners prescribe copious amounts of relaxants and anti-depressants. Relying on medication is like using crutches to walk if your legs are tired. It would be better to put your feet up and rest and then get going again when you feel rejuvenated. Medication may take away the symptoms of stress, but it doesn't examine or deal with the cause. Alternative avenues need to be explored.

Mental Relaxation An important factor in stress control is learning how to relax. To be mentally relaxed you need to look

The often conflicting demands of work and family can be balanced if time is used efficiently.

at your thought patterns under moments of real stress. Pinpoint all your negative responses. (Referring back to your answers in the Automatic Thoughts Questionnaire may assist you here.) Once you have isolated your negative responses, replace them with a more rational and positive approach to that thought. This may be difficult and may take some time, but persevere until you have achieved a different response.

If you know you have a particular way of reacting to a stressful situation, write down that situation on a small card. On the back of the card write a more rational response. Carry it around, look at it often and repeat the rational response to yourself. Gradually you will learn to control your thoughts and when the stressful situation arises the rational response will come automatically to mind.

Mental relaxation will allow you to take constructive steps to control your thoughts rather than allowing them to control you.

A relaxing body stretch in the early morning is a great way to begin the day.

STRESS MANAGEMENT

Physical Relaxation This is just as important for our bodies as exercise. If relaxing seems to you a waste of time which could be better utilised doing something else then you are precisely the person who needs to relax the most. Taking a small amount of time each week to relax will make you more productive and help prevent stress related illness.

To relax your body listen to a relaxation tape regularly. There are a wide range of cassettes commercially available. Select the tape that suits you best. If you prefer you can make your own relaxation tape by taping your own voice reading the following procedure, or ask someone else to read it to you.

(In preparation select a comfortable place that is free of unnecessary noise and any interruptions. Take your telephone off the hook. Put on some quiet music, but make sure it is something you won't have to get up and change for at least ten minutes. Lie on your back with your arms down by your sides and your legs straight. Don't cross your ankles. Put anything you have to do next or later out of your mind and concentrate completely on relaxing. If you want to tape your own voice, you should start the tape now.)

Close your eyes and take a deep breath, in through the nose, out through the mouth... Once again take a deep breath in, feel your chest rise, breath out.

Relax all the muscles of the body, starting with your facial muscles. Relax your shoulders, all of your arms, right down to your wrists and fingers. Relax your stomach muscles, your bottom muscles, all of your legs, right down to your ankles and toes.

Completely relax... You will know you are really relaxed when you begin to feel very heavy, as though you could imagine yourself sinking right through the floor.

Once more take a deep breath in... and breathe out.

Now just think about your head. Slowly, very slowly, roll your head over to the left shoulder and let it flop there. As you are now so heavy and relaxed even this small movement will feel like a big effort. Now roll your head over to the right shoulder and just let it drop there by your shoulder. Just relax there for a moment.

Feel relaxed. Slowly roll your head back to the centre.

Now just think about your arms. Slowly tighten all of your arms, clench your fists and hold these muscles really hard. Hold for four counts — 1, 2, 3, 4 — now relax. Make sure you are once again completely relaxed including your wrists and fingers.

This time think about your stomach. Squeeze your stomach up and underneath the rib cage, hold it there so your stomach has a hollow area. Once again hold for the count of four — 1, 2, 3, 4 — now relax all of the stomach muscles... completely relax. Take a deep breath in... hold it... breathe out.

Last of all, just think about your legs. Tighten all of your legs. Start with the quads, tighten them, your calves, point your toes hard down towards the floor. Hold this position really tightly, so tight you feel all your muscles shaking. Hold it still very tight... now relax.

Relax all of the body completely. Just lie there and let your imagination wander. Take yourself to a place which means total relaxation to you. Just imagine that you are there. Feel the surroundings, the elements and the pleasant feelings you have. Just lie there and enjoy it. Count back from ten to one — 10, 9, 8, 7, 6, 5, 4, 3, 2, 1.
Now slowly think about where you are.

Slowly open your eyes. Take the peaceful relaxed feeling with you for the rest of the day.

TACKLING SOME COMMON CAUSES OF STRESS

You It is easy to blame external factors, but how much of the stress you experience is your own fault?

Particular kinds of people are more prone to stress than others. They have very high expectations of themselves. They also place a great deal of importance on being liked or receiving attention from others. The stress-prone person is usually in a rush and tries to fit a multitude of things into a limited time period.

Think of an aspect of your own behaviour that fits into this category and aim to change it. It's much easier to tackle one point at a time.

Stress is not something only adults are afflicted with. Children as young as primary school age can also be affected by stress. The most common cause of stress for children is a low sense of self worth. It is important to teach your children methods of dealing with stress similar to those you are learning yourself.

Work If you spend a large percentage of your life at work it is essential that it provides some enjoyment and sense of achievement. The structure of work is actually becoming more stressful in society today. Increased specialisation has meant that work is now more repetitive at some levels. A worker may never see the finished product they contribute to. A manager may have no 'hands on' experience or person-to-person contact with their staff.

Aim to make the most out of every situation and opportunity that presents itself. Maintain good lines of communication. Let your supervisors know what you are doing, what you have achieved and where your goals lie. Continually strive to improve your knowledge and skills. Proceed at a pace that matches your ability. Once we are comfortable in our job we often become reluctant to take new risks. Be ambitious and not afraid of change.

Relationships It is common to experience stress with those who are close to you. At different stages of our lives our goals may change. You may need to readjust some of your life goals to those of your partner. Women today have more choices in their lives. They tend to marry later and have fewer children.

Don't let the whole of your spare time become devoted to your children. It is worth the expense to have a night out with your partner every now and then. This ensures that you still know each other and feel cared about.

Money Money is often said to be the root of all evil, but handled well, it can be the source of much pleasure and happiness. Financial stress occurs once you want or maybe have more than you can really afford. Because of the power of advertising this situation can happen almost without us realising it.

Devising a working budget for yourself is the most positive step you can take. It is essential whether you are a millionaire or on the breadline. Credit cards can be your worst enemy. They are particularly nasty for the impulsive buyer who makes decisions on the spur of the moment. If your credit cards control you, destroy them. They may not be worth the stress. Make sure you incorporate the high credit card interest rates into your working budget.

STRESS AND YOUR BODY

Another area of our lives we can take direct action on to relieve stress is our body. If we need a financial incentive, the money saved on doctor's bills, decreased productivity, periods of sickness and lack of creativity and motivation would be enormous. A well-tuned body is far more capable of dealing with inevitable excess stress. A fit body is not only physically healthy, it is psychologically healthy.

Stress Management

People who are prone to stress are always in a hurry.

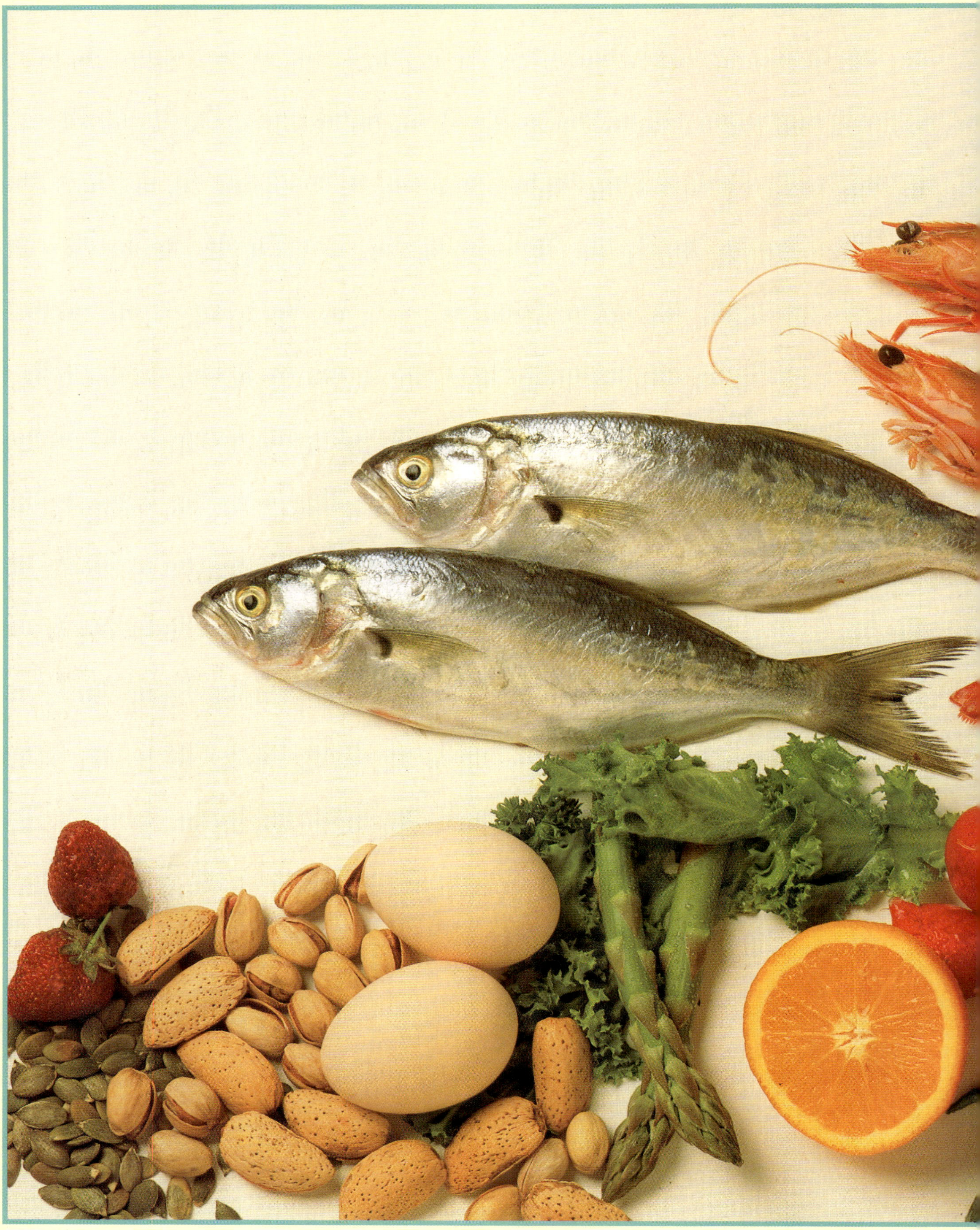

CHAPTER FOUR

FOOD FOR HEALTH AND FITNESS

SENSIBLE EATING HABITS AND REGULAR EXERCISE WILL DEVELOP A BODY SHAPE THAT IS RIGHT FOR YOU

The aim of this section is to make you nutritionally aware. Every time you eat something, you should know what it is and exactly how it is going to affect your body.

NUTRIENTS

What exactly happens to the food we eat is explained by the digestive process.

Our sandwich or breakfast cereal is first digested and then absorbed. It is turned into small molecules of the major nutrients. These groups of nutrients include proteins, carbohydrates, fats, vitamins, minerals, water and dietary fibre.

Carbohydrates These are the principal energy foods and should form a major part (about 60%) of our food. There are two types of carbohydrates, called simple and complex. The first type is called simple because the chemical molecule is small and therefore easily digested. The simple carbohydrates are classified as sugars and include glucose, fructose (from fruit and vegetables), sucrose (from cane sugar) and lactose (from milk).

Complex carbohydrates are classified as starches and are found in foods such as cereals, potatoes, bread and grains. They are also broken down to glucose, but the digestive process takes longer as the chemical molecule is larger. Complex carbohydrates also contain other nutrients, while simple ones do not.

Glucose is our principal fuel food. It provides the muscles with energy and also fuels other bodily functions such as breathing and digesting. After glucose is absorbed it is carried to the liver and from there via the bloodstream to the muscles for immediate use or storage as glycogen. Glucose in excess of this storage capacity is converted to fat and stored in the fat tissues under the skin.

Proteins These should comprise about 20% of food intake. Proteins are relatively complex chemical molecules and contain the essential element nitrogen. Proteins are built up or synthesised from amino acids, which are contained in the foods we eat. There are more than 20 amino acids of which eight are essential to life. In response to a need for a particular protein (for example, to restore damaged tissue or to promote growth) the liver assembles the 'recipe' of amino acids, which are required in the correct proportions.

The replacement of the body's cells is one function of proteins, another is the production of the enzymes used in digestion. Amino acids cannot be stored and must therefore form part of the daily food intake. Excess protein is converted to fat and stored.

Fats These should comprise about 20% of our food intake. Fat is also used as fuel. It is not as readily available to the muscles as glucose because it is relatively difficult to break down, especially in inactive people. Fats are used in the building of new cells, to insulate nerves and vital organs, and in the production of hormones. Australians generally eat too much fat and the excess is stored under the skin.

Vitamins Vitamins are small molecules that are needed by the body in much smaller quantities, about

1% of food intake. They interact with other nutrients to regulate many of the body's functions. Thirteen vitamins are essential to health.

Minerals These are needed in much the same quantities as vitamins and act with them to regulate many body functions and chemical processes. They are responsible for building the body's bone structure.

Water Water constitutes 60% of the body and is therefore the most essential nutrient. It is lost through urine, sweat, the lungs and faeces, and must be replaced. Drinking fluids and eating foods with a higher water content, such as fruit and vegetables, replaces lost body water.

Dietary Fibre Although not strictly a nutrient, dietary fibre is essential in our food because it absorbs water and helps speed up the movement of food along the digestive tract. High fibre diets are linked with a low incidence of coronary heart disease, bowel cancer and diabetes. It also increases the availability of vitamins and minerals. Fibre is found in cereal foods, fruits and vegetables.

A balanced diet should contain plenty of carbohydrates (above) and fresh fruit (left).

BALANCED FOOD INTAKE

Though tempting to the eye and palate, these foods do not supply the essential nutrients.

Once we are aware of the presence of nutrients it is important to understand the nutrient composition of the food we eat. Most foods contain more than one nutrient, but the composition and proportions differ from food to food. For a balanced food intake we should choose those foods that represent the best combination of nutrient content and kilojoules. Kilojoules measure the amount of energy that food is capable of generating. This was formerly measured in calories (4.2 kilojoules = 1 calorie), and calorie equivalents are given throughout the book.

Be wary of 'empty' foods. These provide energy in the form of kilojoules, but do not supply the essential nutrients. Sugar products such as soft drink, biscuits, and alcohol are foods in this category. Although they provide us with an instant energy boost, this is followed by fatigue and lethargy. Today many food products display both the kilojoule content and the nutrient composition on the label.

Foods are generally classified into five groups. These are described with the nutrients they contain:

GROUP	NUTRIENTS	DAILY INTAKE
BREADS AND CEREALS	complex carbohydrate protein Vitamin B_1 (thiamine) dietary fibre	1 cup of cereal* 4 slices wholegrain bread
FRUIT AND VEGETABLES	complex carbohydrate simple fruit sugars (fructose) protein dietary fibre Vitamin A (retinol) Vitamin C (ascorbic acid) Folic Acid	2 servings of fruit 4 servings of vegetables
MILK AND CHEESE PRODUCTS	protein Vitamin A Vitamin B_2 (riboflavin) Vitamin D fat	300 ml of milk or 40 g of cheese or 1 small yoghurt
MEAT AND MEAT ALTERNATIVES	protein Vitamin B_1 (thiamine) Vitamin B_3 (niacin) fat iron	1 medium serving lean meat or legumes or nuts
FATS AND OILS**	fat Vitamin A Vitamin D Vitamin E	1 tablespoon butter or equivalent

* Be wary of processed breakfast cereals with increased sugar content. Check the labels.

**Choose these foods wisely, particularly if whole milk and meat have also been included in daily intake.

QUICK ENERGY

If you think chocolate is going to give you a quick energy boost — think again. The rise in blood sugar associated with eating chocolate, or drinking high sugar drinks (e.g. cordial or soft drinks) results in lower than usual blood sugar. You will feel shaky and weak resulting in low performance.

NUTRIENT DEFICIENCY

As no food group can provide all essential nutrients, it is necessary to choose daily from each of the five food groups listed. Continually eating food with little nutrient content, especially fast food and takeaways, can lead to health problems. Listed below are nutrient deficiencies common in Australia, and the best food sources to help avoid them.

BREAKFAST LIKE A KING

Breakfast is the most important meal of the day. You should eat a large breakfast including fruit juice, quality cereal and skim milk (for those watching their diet), boiled egg on toast, yoghurt and fruit.

NUTRIENT	SYMPTOM	BEST FOOD SOURCES
VITAMIN A (retinol)	night blindness, decreased resistance to skin and mucous membrane infection	liver, cod liver oil, carrots, parsley, spinach
VITAMIN B_1 (thiamine)	tiredness, irritability, depressed appetite*	yeast, nuts
VITAMIN B_{12} (cobalamin)	pernicious anaemia	liver, kidney, sardines, oysters
VITAMIN C (ascorbic acid)	increased susceptibility to infections, increased healing time	blackcurrants, citrus fruit, capsicum
CALCIUM	fragility of bones, dental diseases, may contribute to high blood pressure	milk and milk products
IRON	anaemia, fatigue	meat, liver
IODINE	enlargement of thyroid gland	seafood, iodised salt
MAGNESIUM	controls muscle contractions and nerve functioning (together with calcium, potassium and sodium)	nuts, vegetables, flour, bread
ZINC	helps metabolise carbohydrate and protein, as well as speeding up the healing of cuts and sores	meat, seafood, eggs, milk, nuts, whole grains, pulses

* Note. Alcohol reduces the body's reserves of thiamine.

NUTRIENT DEFICIENCIES SPECIAL TO WOMEN

BEST SOURCES OF IRON	BEST SOURCES OF VITAMIN C
all red meat, chicken, fish, legumes, wholemeal bread, dried fruit, spinach (all plant sources of iron need Vitamin C for effective absorption).	guavas, capsicums, blackcurrants parsley, broccoli (cooked), brussel sprouts (cooked), paw paw, strawberries, cabbage, orange juice, mangoes, grapefruit, lemon juice, redcurrants, radish, spinach (cooked), lime juice, mandarines, chilli sauce, lambs liver

Iron Deficiency This condition produces an anaemia in women who do not have sufficient iron in their food to meet their daily needs. The symptoms are a general feeling of lethargy, fatigue and loss of appetite, and in an athlete, a reduction in performance. Because iron is lost during the menstrual cycle, menstruating women need to replace it. Female endurance athletes are particularly at risk due to both increased iron loss and reduced iron absorption in the digestive tract.

The risk of iron deficiency is reduced by making dietary choices of foods high in iron. Iron is found in both plant and animal products. However, the iron in animal products (haem iron) is more readily absorbed from the digestive tract. A female vegetarian is at greater risk than a non-vegetarian. When Vitamin C is ingested along with foods containing iron, it aids the absorption of iron from the digestive tract.

Osteoporosis This is a condition by which bone density is decreased by calcium loss. Twenty-five per cent of women over the age of 60 are affected by osteoporosis. It causes the shrinkage in height common in many elderly people, and is responsible for their susceptibility to fractures, particularly in the hip, and the condition known as 'Dowager's Hump'.

Up to about the age of 40, calcium is deposited relatively easily in the bones. Then calcium is gradually lost. This process speeds up in women after menopause, because of the decrease in the hormone oestrogen, which plays a role in body calcium levels. The amount of exercise is also generally reduced with age. Exercise such as walking or running has been shown to activate the process of bone formation, and is an important component of bone health.

Apart from post-menstrual women there are several groups of women at risk from low calcium stores. Pregnant women and breastfeeding mothers use their own calcium to provide sufficient for the bone health of their child. Athletes and ballet dancers whose body fat is very low are also at risk from loss in bone density. This occurs when the intensity of training causes them to stop menstruating (called athletic amenorrhea), resulting in a disruption in the ability of oestrogen to regulate calcium levels. The amenorrhea accompanying anorexia nervosa produces the same effects. Finally, women who drink alcohol or smoke heavily are also at risk.

> **It is advisable to begin an exercise program before you make any alterations to your food intake, so that the increase in your metabolic rate can occur first. By then decreasing your energy intake you will accelerate loss of unwanted fat.**

There are two ways to prevent osteoporosis, most effectively done before 35 years of age.

- Ensure that calcium intake through diet is high in the years up to age 35, and that this is continued throughout life. Calcium intake should be approximately 800 mg per day, increasing to 1100 mg when pregnant and 1200 mg when breastfeeding. Post-menopausal women should aim for a daily intake of about 1000 mg.
- Ensure that weight-bearing exercise such as walking or jogging forms an integral part of your lifestyle.

There are some other steps you can take to improve your bone health. Spending some time in the sunshine increases your Vitamin D levels. This helps the absorption of calcium from the digestive tract. Keep salt, caffeine and protein levels within the normal limits. These substances increase the amount of calcium lost from the body in urine.

Prevention of osteoporosis is better than cure. However, calcium supplements and oestrogen therapy may be necessary for people who are unable to include calcium rich foods in their diets. Check with your doctor before you embark on either program.

Pregnant women are at risk from low calcium stores.

BEST SOURCES OF CALCIUM

All dairy products, such as milk (calcium content remains the same regardless of whether the milk is high or low in fat), yoghurt and cheese (cottage cheese does not contain as much calcium as hard cheese); sardines; broccoli; sesame seeds.

NB Calcium from dairy products is more readily absorbed than calcium from plant products.

WEIGHT CONTROL

As well as maintaining a correct balance of nutrients in our food, we must ensure that we monitor our kilojoule intake. When excess kilojoules are eaten over and above those needed to provide energy, the body stores them as fat. The pattern of fat deposition varies between females and males. Generally, females deposit fat in the lower part of the body (hips and thighs) and males deposit fat on the upper body (especially the stomach).

When we see fat children with fat parents it is easy to attribute this to genetic or hereditary factors. This is usually not the case. Fat children are the product of poor eating patterns imposed by their parents and usually accompanied by negative attitudes to exercise.

★ ★ ★

The term cellulite is often used to describe fat deposits, particularly in females. Cellulite is no different from other storage fat, and its deposition and removal are subject to the same principles that apply to fat. It is not possible to perform particular exercises to spot reduce (for example, sit-ups to remove abdominal fat). The body removes fat evenly from all the fat stores. Beware advertising campaigns that promise to spot reduce. Vibrator belts have no benefit whatsoever and plastic wraps or suits can be a potential health hazard because they induce dehydration of the body.

Although advertising campaigns would have us believe that every woman should be a 'perfect size 10', many of us simply do not fall into this category. Through sensible eating patterns and a commitment to regular exercise it is possible to develop and keep a body shape that is right for you.

The basic plan for weight control is a very simple one. It is called the energy balance equation:

Blend your favourite fruits with either skim milk or water, add wheatgerm, and an egg if you want extra protein, some cinnamon, and sprinkle nutmeg on top for a great drink. Drink as a snack or use as a quick meal. (For a meal replacement add plenty of fruit).

2 bananas
1 cup strawberries
wheatgerm
egg (optional)
1 teaspoon cinnamon
2 cups skim milk
Blend — add in nutmeg

★ ★ ★

A portion of rockmelon chopped
4 almonds
2 tablespoons raw muesli
1 teaspoon honey
1 teaspoon sesame seeds
Sprinkle nutmeg
Add milk or soya milk to cover in blender

---

energy input = energy output
or
food eaten = energy expended
(in kilojoules)   (in kilojoules)

An imbalance in this equation results in people who are overweight. They simply eat more kilojoules than they expend in energy. If you wish to maintain weight, then the balance implied in this equation should be adopted daily. If you wish to reduce weight, then energy output must be greater than energy input. If you wish to gain weight, energy input must be greater than energy output.

DAILY INTAKE KILOJOULE(CALORIE)	DAILY EXPENDITURE KILOJOULE(CALORIE)	
10 885(2600)	10 885(2600)	= Stable weight
12 560(3000) Overeating	10 885(2600)	= Weight gain
9210(2200)	12 140(2900)	= Weight loss

METABOLISM

If the above is the basic equation for weight loss, why is it that some people can eat as much as they like and not put on weight, while others seemingly only have to 'look at food' and they gain weight? The answer is that different people expend energy at different rates. The process by which energy is made available in each body cell is called metabolism. Metabolism of kilojoules continues even while we are asleep to maintain our essential functions. The rate at which metabolism occurs under these circumstances is called our Basal Metabolic Rate (BMR). Some people have a high BMR, while others have a low or slower BMR. This affects how quickly your body burns fat. You can calculate your own BMR by using the following formula:

21.6 × body weight (in kilograms) =
...... kilojoules per day
For example a 60 kilogram woman would require
1296 kilojoules per day
simply to maintain
basic body functions.
(21.6 × 60 = 1296)

METABOLISM AND EXERCISE

When the body is not sleeping, the intensity of the activity will determine the metabolic rate. Kilojoules expended vary with the intensity of the activity. A simple analogy is the way the accelerator in a motor car varies the rate at which fuel is used by the engine. The higher the acceleration the greater the fuel usage and the faster the car moves. As the duration and intensity of an activity increases, the person performing the activity is utilising more kilojoules to continue the exercise. In addition, the metabolic rate of someone who exercises stays higher than normal (for up to 24 hours) even after that person has finished exercising.

The table opposite lists some common sports and domestic activities with their approximate metabolic costs for a 60 kilogram woman:

> An exercise program may increase muscle weight and at the same time reduce fat weight. This is called body toning, and it is characterised by a decrease in body fat, particularly on the legs and arms. When this fat, which usually covers the muscles, is removed, the underlying muscle layer acquires greater definition. You can see the outline of individual muscles more clearly. The muscles are not necessarily getting bigger, just more obvious. This is generally more aesthetically pleasing than heavy limbs and body covered with fat.

Food for Health and Fitness

SPORTING ACTIVITY	KILOJOULES (CALORIES) PER 5 MINUTES
athletics	147(35)
badminton	105–126(25–30)
circuit training	210(50)
climbing/hill walking	147(35)
cross country running	189–210(45–50)
cycling (slow)	84(20)
cycling (fast)	126–210(30–50)
gymnastics	84–105(20–25)
horse riding	126(30)
ice-skating	105(25)
karate	126(30)
netball	126(30)
roller skating	63–84(15–20)
rowing (slow)	84(20)
running (slow jogging)	126–158(30–38)
sailing	63–126(15–30)
skiing (downhill)	126–147(30–35)
skiing (cross country)	252(60)
skipping	210(50)
squash	252(60)
swimming (slow)	168(40)
swimming (competitive)	189–210(45–50)
table tennis	84(20)
tennis	126(30)
walking (strolling)	63–84(15–20)
walking (fast)	105–126(25–30)
waterskiing	126–147(30–35)
windsurfing	126–147(30–35)
yoga	63(15)

DOMESTIC ACTIVITY	KILOJOULES (CALORIES) PER 5 MINUTES
bedmaking	63(15)
car washing	84(20)
cleaning cupboards	42(10)
cleaning floors/windows	63(15)
cooking	42(10)
dancing (ballroom)	63(15)
dancing (disco)	126–147(30–35)
driving a car	42(10)
dusting	42(10)
gardening (heavy)	155(37)
gardening (light)	63–84(15–20)
home decorating	42–63(10–15)
ironing	42(10)
knitting and sewing	29(7)
polishing (furniture)	63(15)
shopping	42(10)
typewriting	29–42(7–10)
vacuum cleaning	15(3)
washing dishes	42(10)
washing clothes by hand	63(15)

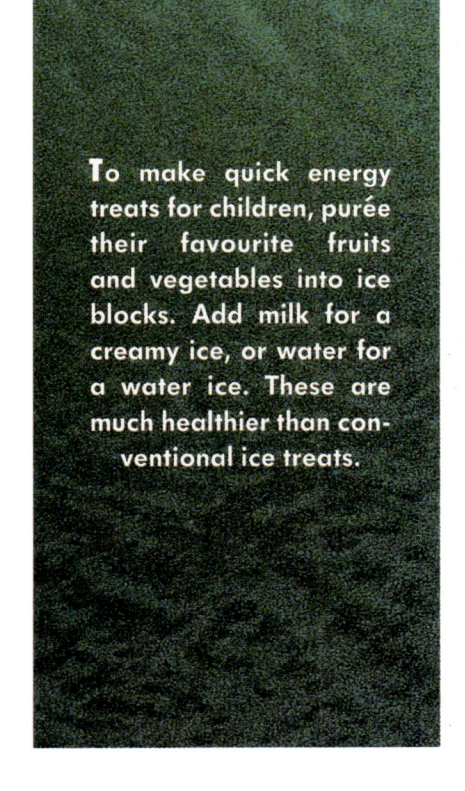

There are many factors that affect BMR. Muscle tissue has a higher metabolic rate than fat tissue. Therefore, once a person has toned up and lost unwanted fat through exercise they burn more kilojoules performing everyday activities. BMR also decreases with age, by approximately 2% every ten years. As we get older, meal size should decrease to avoid weight gain.

To maintain your current body weight you need to ensure that the total daily kilojoules you eat equals the

> To make quick energy treats for children, purée their favourite fruits and vegetables into ice blocks. Add milk for a creamy ice, or water for a water ice. These are much healthier than conventional ice treats.

total kilojoules used in energy. If you wish to lose weight your energy input must be less than your energy output. A realistic weight loss would be half a kilogram per week. In order to lose this amount, the daily difference between energy input and energy output would need to be 2100 kilojoules(501 calories). There are three ways to achieve this:

a reduce food intake by 2100 kilojoules(501 calories), or

b increase energy output through exercise by 2100 kilojoules (501 calories), or

c reduce food intake and increase exercise output by a combined total of 2100 kilojoules (501 calories).

Of these alternatives the most effective method is **c**. To take option **a** is difficult as it is often accompanied by hunger pangs. This leads you quickly back into your former eating patterns. Your minimum daily intake needs to be approximately 5000 kilojoules (1199 calories) and to drop below this compromises nutrition, particularly vitamin and mineral intake. Option **b** requires a volume of exercise that many would find difficult to sustain daily. Option **c** allows you to reduce food intake and to combine this with an exercise program.

The key to success in adopting option **c** is to develop the self discipline required to incorporate these two aspects into your lifestyle. There is no easy, magic recipe for weight loss. It requires a life-long commitment, practised daily, to watch what you eat and to get your body moving.

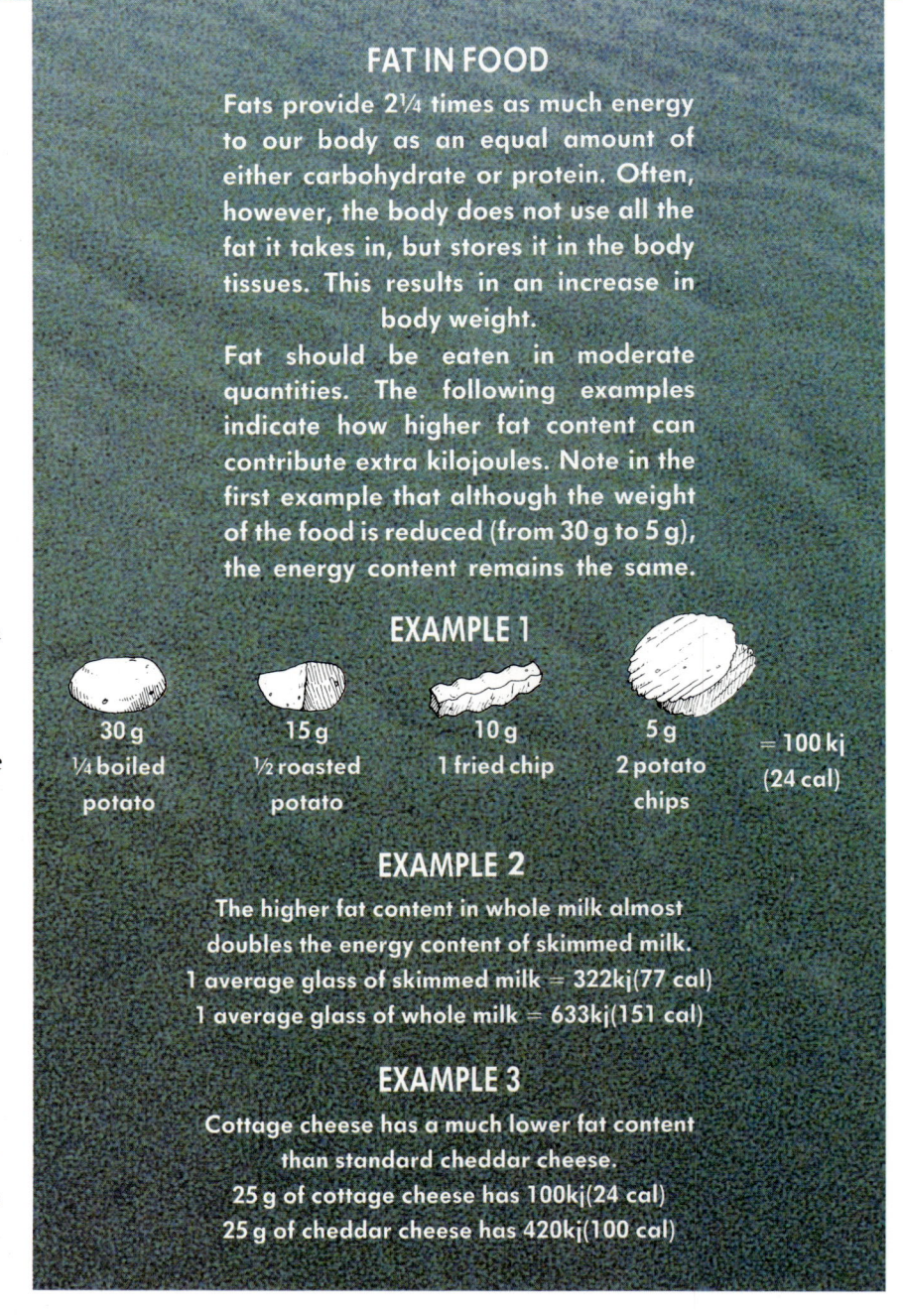

FAT IN FOOD

Fats provide 2¼ times as much energy to our body as an equal amount of either carbohydrate or protein. Often, however, the body does not use all the fat it takes in, but stores it in the body tissues. This results in an increase in body weight.

Fat should be eaten in moderate quantities. The following examples indicate how higher fat content can contribute extra kilojoules. Note in the first example that although the weight of the food is reduced (from 30 g to 5 g), the energy content remains the same.

EXAMPLE 1

30 g	15 g	10 g	5 g	
¼ boiled potato	½ roasted potato	1 fried chip	2 potato chips	= 100 kj (24 cal)

EXAMPLE 2

The higher fat content in whole milk almost doubles the energy content of skimmed milk.
1 average glass of skimmed milk = 322kj(77 cal)
1 average glass of whole milk = 633kj(151 cal)

EXAMPLE 3

Cottage cheese has a much lower fat content than standard cheddar cheese.
25 g of cottage cheese has 100kj(24 cal)
25 g of cheddar cheese has 420kj(100 cal)

IDEAL WEIGHT

Many popular magazines regularly publish height–weight scales to allow the reader to determine whether they are the 'ideal weight'. Such an approach ignores your level of body fat. You will probably learn more about your body by looking in the mirror. A better way to determine your ideal weight is to give yourself a simple pinch test. Take hold of a skinfold about 2 cm to the right of your navel. If that skinfold is greater than 2 cm then you are carrying more body fat than is ideal. Try the same in the centre of your thigh, behind your upper arm, or just above your hip bone.

When you adopt a balanced exercise and eating program you will notice that the fat in these places will gradually be reduced. Don't expect magical results overnight. Checking changes in body fat every 4–6 weeks is the best way to monitor your progress. This will tell you more about changes in your body composition than regularly weighing yourself on the bathroom scales. In fact, it is possible to gain weight on the scales, yet see a significant reduction in body fat, accompanied by a decrease in clothing size. The reason for this apparent contradiction is that muscle tissue actually weighs more than fat tissue.

UNDERSTANDING DIETS

We often interpret the word 'diet' as referring to a special eating plan. A diet is something one 'goes on', and logically then 'comes off' at some later stage. Most of us at some time have tried a diet plan with usually limited success. Diet plans suggested in the popular press can be grouped according to their overall principles:

fasting	(very little or no food at all)
single food	(e.g. grapefruit diet)
high protein	(e.g. Scarsdale Diet)
high carbohydrate	(e.g. Beverly Hills Diet)

Once you understand the nutritional needs of your body you realise that none of these diets satisfactorily meet the daily requirements in one or more nutrient

EATING ON THE RUN

If you are late and do not have time to eat, don't make do with a cup of coffee. Grab some fruit, a tub of yoghurt or even some plain fresh bread — anything is better than nothing.

If you have to eat something quick and convenient for lunch, try a salad sandwich and fresh juice.

Good nutritional habits can be followed even when you are 'on the run'.

> ## VEGETABLES
>
> These are great sources of vitamins, minerals, trace elements, natural sugars and fibre. They are low in kilojoules, full of carbohydrates and have no cholesterol. Raw vegetables are best for nutritional value. Buy your fresh vegetables as you need them — stocking up on the weekends at the local market may be economical, but vegetables soon lose their goodness stored in a fridge. Canned vegetables have little nutritional value.
>
> When cooking vegetables, keep the water, as it contains many vitamins and minerals. Use it for soups or vegetable drinks.
>
> ### VEGETABLE PIE
> Chop all your favourite vegetables, and cook lightly. Add soya beans, pine nuts, and vegemite. Cook potatoes and mash. Top vegetable mix with mash. Add paprika and low fat cheese (optional). Bake for a great pie.

groups. Your body must receive sufficient carbohydrates, protein, fat, vitamins, minerals, water and fibre every day. In addition these diets are often difficult to fit into your lifestyle and more expensive than a normal balanced diet. Dieters may see a change in weight on the scales, but this can be attributed to a decrease in body water not fat.

These fad diets can often only be maintained over a short period. The body quickly craves the nutrients the diet is lacking, and those who have not learned to interpret these signals correctly, usually respond by binge eating. Another reason for their failure is the 'set point' theory. This suggests that the body's metabolic rate is different for each of us. This is in turn related to a set point in the size of the body's fat store. When the kilojoule intake is drastically reduced the metabolic rate is lowered so that the fat reserves remain relatively constant. When you come off the diet and your kilojoule intake is increased the metabolic rate does not respond quickly. This results in a weight gain at a faster rate than before the diet.

The secret to successful weight control is not which diet plan you follow, but that you have an overall eating plan. This plan should be one that is easily incorporated into your lifestyle and which is based on your understanding of sound nutritional principles. Throw away your diet books and spend some time learning the kilojoule equivalents of the food you eat. Occasionally eating something that is 'bad' for you won't do you any harm provided you follow two simple rules:

- you obtain the necessary nutrients daily
- the kilojoules eaten are in keeping with your weight control goals

> ## KNOWING WHAT YOU EAT
>
> There are several types of computer programs that analyse your dietary intake. The program sets your personal nutrition goals, including kilojoules, fat, protein, carbohydrates, vitamins and minerals. It will also give you a full breakdown in figures and graphic descriptions of your food intake. Ask a nutritionist or an instructor at your local gym for this program.

EATING PATTERNS

Learning when to eat can be more complicated than it sounds. Our eating patterns are conditioned by many things including time of day, the [...] moods and social occasion[...]

Dieters often believe tha[...] lishing sound practices. The [...] The fast produces hunger and [...] binge eating. It is necessary t[...] and behaviours that have the [...] overeating and replace them w[...] habits. Here are some hints to he[...] energy equation:

- eat slowly
- eat only at a specific place in you[...] should be as attractive as possible.
- don't eat while you are engaged in other activities, such as watching television
- do not keep jars of biscuits or sweets
- schedule an exercise session late in the afternoon to reduce your appetite at dinner time
- eat smaller meals more regularly
- keep in mind the following:
    - breakfast like a king
    - lunch like a prince
    - dine like a pauper

EATING OUT

Eating out can be fairly hazardous for someone trying to control their weight. Fast foods have a very high fat content with little nutritional value. At restaurants there is a tendency to consume far more food than we really need. Consider the average restaurant meal: entrée, accompanied by bread, main course, dessert

BEST TAKE-AWAYS

ITALIAN
Ask for the sauce to be placed in a separate container so that you can control how much is used. Pasta by itself is not fattening.

MEXICAN
Add refried beans to tortilla shells and pile high with salad. This is a low kilojoule alternative to corn chips smothered in cheese, sour cream and avocado!

CHINESE
Ask for food without M.S.G. Choose vegetable mixes and rice. Avoid Chinese dishes that are deep fried — these will add many kilojoules.

HOT BREAD KITCHENS
These are full of tempting goodies. Bran muffins can be good, but check the ingredients with your local bakery. A freshly baked bread roll with nothing added can also be delicious. I started to buy them on the way home from training and the smell was so enticing, I ate them before I got home and had time to add butter.

RESTAURANTS
If eating out regularly, choose low kilojoule meals. Ask for salad dressing and sauces to be served separately. Use sparingly. Go easy on the desserts. A three-course meal plus garlic bread, coffee and chocolate can use about two days quota of kilojoules. Eat lightly the day following and exercise at least 1–2 hours at moderate pace to help maintain weight.

Best food choices at restaurants: grilled lean meat, chicken, fish, vegetables (without butter), baked potato (not fattening on its own — try yoghurt and herbs instead of butter)

PRE RACE/EVENT FOOD

Always experiment with food before race day. Never eat anything you are not used to eating the day before or hours before your event.

The day before you compete is a crucial day nutritionally, as the foods you eat will help sustain you through your event. Also drink plenty of water — until your urine is clear. Remember to drink before, during and after your event. If your event is short, do not drink so much that you feel bloated — sip water slowly hours before.

Eat a balanced diet, including plenty of fruits, bread and vegetables.

On race day, eat a carbohydrate meal at least 2–3 hours before the start of your event. This will keep you satisfied but also allow time for digestion. Avoid high fibre or spicy foods, which could cause stomach ache.

BEST CHOICES
Sandwiches with plain filling (only a little butter)
Spaghetti or any pasta (little sauce)
Baked potatoes with herbs and lemon to taste
Rice — brown and wild are best
Grilled fish
Fruit salad
Fresh juices

WORST CHOICES
Deep fried foods
Convenience foods (e.g. hamburgers, chips, chocolates, cake, lollies, ice blocks)
Soft drinks
Steak

---

and coffee, not to mention the drinks. This can amount to a full day's kilojoule allowance, sometimes more. It is no wonder that you put on weight if you eat out several times a week with little or no exercise.

There are some ways to control the effects of eating out. If possible go out for lunch instead of dinner, and walk back to work. Try to exercise before a large meal to reduce your appetite. Make low kilojoule choices from the menu. If you are going out to dinner, make sure you eat lightly during the day and on the following day.

FOOD FOR SPORT

Your training diet should also conform to sound nutritional principles. It is important that the energy balance equation is maintained. This is true regardless of the level of activity — whether you are sedentary, exercise 3 times a week, or 3 times a day.

The major difference between the serious athlete and the health-conscious jogger is the energy requirement. The athlete needs a higher kilojoule intake because of a higher kilojoule output. The demands of training may also alter nutrient requirements. This would vary from sport to sport, and would be determined by the frequency, intensity and duration of training sessions. No magic recipe exists for an ideal training diet. If the athlete understands both the needs of their own sport and good nutrition, then he or she can devise their own training diet plan to incorporate food that they like and that is practical to prepare.

It is advisable for an athlete to choose a nutritious diet from a variety of foods. They should cut down on fat and sugar, limit the use of alcohol, use less salt and increase consumption of wholegrain bread, cereals, vegetables and fruit. One of the most important nutrients that everyone, but especially athletes, need

FOOD FOR HEALTH AND FITNESS

Hand – held water weights double as a convenient source of fluid while exercising.

to ensure is in their diet in copious quantities is water. Water is necessary before, during and after activity to maintain the body's fluid balance.

Breakfast is an essential part of any training diet. It ensures that your glycogen stores are fully replaced from the morning training session. It provides carbohydrates for readily available energy during the day's activity and the afternoon session. If you don't eat any or enough breakfast you will fatigue more easily and lose concentration, be hungry later when good breakfast foods are unavailable and consequently consume higher fat or sugar snack foods, and you will eat too much at night before bed when you won't digest it properly.

BEST BREAKFAST FOODS

FRUIT Fresh, unsweetened tinned, juice, dried (but has a high sugar content).

CEREAL Look for the best ones. According to *Choice* magazine, the five top breakfast cereals (in descending order) are Uncle Toby's Oats, Uncle Toby's Vita-Brits, Uncle Toby's Weeties, Plain Wrap (GJ Coles) Wheat Flakes and Sanitarium Weet-Bix.

BREAD Wholemeal, wholegrain or rye with a small amount of butter/margarine and a light spread, e.g. vegemite. Alternatives to plain bread are muffins, raisin bread, wholemeal pancakes, tinned wholemeal spaghetti.

MILK Low fat (Trim, Hi Lo, Shape, Skim).

If you have time or a higher energy requirement you can add:

PROTEIN Eggs (boiled, poached, scrambled), baked beans, cheese (low fat or thin slices), fish (grilled or canned, e.g. sardines), lean meat (small serve of ham, trimmed bacon, lean mince).

CHOLESTEROL

Cholesterol is a chemical substance formed from fat and is a necessary component in several body functions. When we eat fats (mostly animal fats), we ingest more than we need. The extra cholesterol is deposited on the walls of blood vessels and over time can eventually block the blood vessel, a symptom of coronary heart disease.

Cholesterol is transported in the blood by two chemical carriers, LDLs (Low Density Lipoproteins) and HDLs (High Density Lipoproteins), distinguished, as their names suggest, by the weight of the particles. LDL carries the cholesterol to the walls of the blood vessels. HDL takes cholesterol away from the blood vessels and removes it from the body. Therefore, it is advantageous to reduce LDL cholesterol and to increase the HDL form for optimal heart health.

To reduce LDL cholesterol it is necessary to limit your intake of animal fats. Other things to be avoided include smoking, the high-dose contraceptive pill, some blood pressure medications and being overweight. Research, most of which has been conducted with runners, has shown that regular exercise can increase HDL cholesterol.

The National Heart Foundation recommends a total blood cholesterol of 5.5 millimoles. Get your doctor to check your level annually.

THE HEALTHY DIET PYRAMID

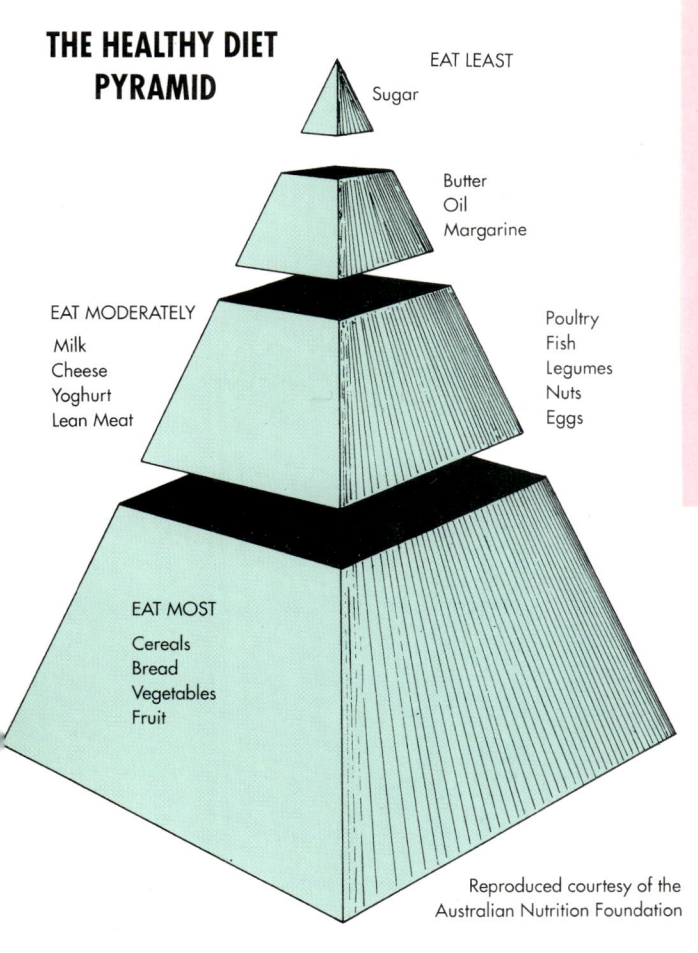

EAT LEAST
Sugar

Butter
Oil
Margarine

EAT MODERATELY
Milk
Cheese
Yoghurt
Lean Meat

Poultry
Fish
Legumes
Nuts
Eggs

EAT MOST
Cereals
Bread
Vegetables
Fruit

Reproduced courtesy of the Australian Nutrition Foundation

A FINAL WORD ON WEIGHT LOSS

The relationship between nutrition, obesity, weight control and exercise is a complex one. Many overweight people are constantly searching for that major recipe which will lead them to their elusive goal — weight loss.

There is no quick, easy solution to weight control. It requires a lifelong commitment, practised daily. Keeping on track requires understanding and controlling those aspects of your lifestyle that may affect your commitment, namely nutrition, exercise, stress reduction and time management.

Set yourself realistic weight loss goals and above all, be patient.

[PRACTICAL WAYS] TO CUT DOWN [FAT CON]SUMPTION

[Handwritten note: Practical ways to cut down fat consumption]

- [Eat smaller cu]ts of red meat, [trim off all fat] and no more than [3 times p]er week.
- [Avoid high]-fat, processed [meats such as l]uncheon meats, [salami, beef] and frankfurts.
- [Remove skin fro]m poultry before [cooking — this cu]ts fat by half.
- Substitute low-fat fish, bean or poultry dishes for red meat.
- Cook all food with minimal fat (e.g. grilled, steamed, baked on a rack or in an oven bag or foil, microwaved, dry fried, lightly stir-fried, barbecued, or casseroled without fat added).
- Never add butter or margarine to food after cooking.
- Avoid creamy sauces and gravies, rich cakes, biscuits and pastry, and oily dressing.
- Substitute low-fat dairy foods for full-fat varieties (e.g. low-fat milk and yoghurt, ricotta and Swiss cheeses).
- Read labels carefully and watch for palm and/or coconut oil in cakes, biscuits, pies and pastries.
- Avoid fried and high-fat food (e.g. French fries, potato and corn chips — 'fast foods').
- Don't use vegetable shortening, this is a hydrogenated fat. Use a combination of 1 part butter/ 1 part safflower oil. Add half the amount of fat called for in a recipe.
- If you eat peanut butter or avocado, use it instead of butter.
- Avoid fatty takeaways and snack foods.

A good way to tell if your body water is at the correct level is to check the colour and odour of your urine. Your urine should be pale yellow in colour (about the colour of lemon juice) and should not have a strong odour. When your body water level is too low your urine will be dark yellow or yellow-brown and will be strong smelling. Note that some vitamin supplements can also cause your urine to be a dark colour and have a strong odour. Always drink before, during, and after exercise. Loss of body water causes fatigue, muscle cramps, and decreases your performance, even in the pool.

CHAPTER FIVE

WELL WATERED

YOUR BODY NEEDS A REGULAR INTAKE OF WATER TO ENABLE IT TO FUNCTION EFFICIENTLY

Picture dried sultanas next to a fresh juicy bunch of grapes. The difference in the same fruit is obvious. The sultanas are the dehydrated body of a once fresh bunch of grapes. The effects of dehydration on the human body are similar, but not quite so apparent.

Our bodies comprise 60% water by volume. An average Australian requires 6-8 glasses of water a day. When you're training you will need at least 12 glasses. Try and incorporate regular water drinking into your normal daily routine. Get into the habit of having a glass of water before each meal, a few glasses of water both before and after a training session and a glass of water first thing in the morning and last thing at night.

During heavy exercise in moderate temperatures (22°C), 2 or 3 litres of sweat can be lost per hour. Only about half this amount can be replaced during exercise. If as little as 2–3% of body weight is lost through dehydration, exercise performance will be impaired. Further fluid loss will seriously compromise your health and could lead to heat injury and death.

Weigh yourself before and after a training session. For every kilo you lose you need to replace about a litre of water. If you don't, it will affect your recovery for the next session.

Remaining properly hydrated enables you to perform at your best by maximising the flow of oxygen and nutrients to the muscle cells and aiding in the efficient removal of the waste products, carbon dioxide and heat.

Our body heats up as we exercise. This heat is dissipated by radiation and conduction from the skin and by the evaporation of sweat. The harder and longer we exercise and the higher the air temperature and humidity, the more limited the body's ability to keep from overheating becomes.

Fortunately the body has an efficient system of recycling water to help guard against dehydration. This system, however, is interfered with by the presence of caffeine or alcohol in the body. These substances act as diuretics, and encourage the body to excrete water, a situation you do not want before exercise. The consumption of sugary alcoholic drinks the night before exercise can result in collapse the next day from dehydration and low blood sugar (hypoglycemia).

To help prevent dehydration and heat injury ensure that you are properly hydrated by drinking 500 ml of cool water 15–30 minutes before exercise. During exercise, replenish the body every 10–15 minutes with 250 ml of water. The weight you lose during exercise is water weight not fat weight. Once you experience thirst your body is already dehydrated.

Avoid endurance training during the heat of the day. Train in the cooler mornings and evenings if daytime temperature exceeds 27°C. Training in water over 30°C will cause the body to overheat.

We need to drink 6–8 glasses of water a day to remain properly hydrated.

Competition organisers should provide adequate water stations every few kilometres of an endurance activity. An event should be cancelled if temperatures exceed 28°Celsius. Individuals must provide their own water during their training sessions. Training routes can be organised to loop around a water supply. Water can be carried on bike frames, in water craft, in waist packs or held in the hand as a water weight. Ensure that the water you drink is not contaminated. Avoid drinking from streams, lakes and dams. If possible filter all drinking water through an activated charcoal filter at home and when travelling, especially overseas.

Training under similar temperatures as those expected on race day can develop some heat acclimatisation. Never restrict water intake during training. To

WELL WATERED

Irrespective of your favourite fitness exercise or activity, be aware of the early warning signs of dehydration and keep your body well watered.

Water is also important if you are trying to lose weight. It helps you digest your food properly and actually stops you retaining fluid by making your kidneys work more effectively. If you do not drink enough every day your body will try and hold onto the water it has. The best fluid to drink is plain, cool water. It quenches your thirst and has no kilojoules. If you don't always like plain water, you can sometimes drink weak cordial, electrolyte drinks or unsweetened fruit juice. You can drink soda water or mineral water with a twist of lemon or lime. Don't drink too much low kilojoule soft drink or cordial as the artificial sweetener is not good for you.

If you are trying to lose weight, fruit juices, fruit drinks and milk drinks should really be considered as foods rather than fluids. They should not be used when you are thirsty. Drinking too little water is also a common cause of accelerated ageing, as the skin becomes dry and more wrinkled.

do so will only risk heat injury. If any of the signs of heat exhaustion develop during training or competition, stop, cool down and rehydrate. Heat stroke is the failure of the body's temperature regulatory system. A high internal body temperature can be fatal. The sufferer may have stopped sweating, appear red and flushed and perhaps even shiver in high temperature. Disorientation and collapse will follow and the situation should be treated as an emergency as the sufferer requires immediate medical attention.

Our bodies comprise 60% water by volume. An average Australian requires 6–8 glasses of water a day.

59

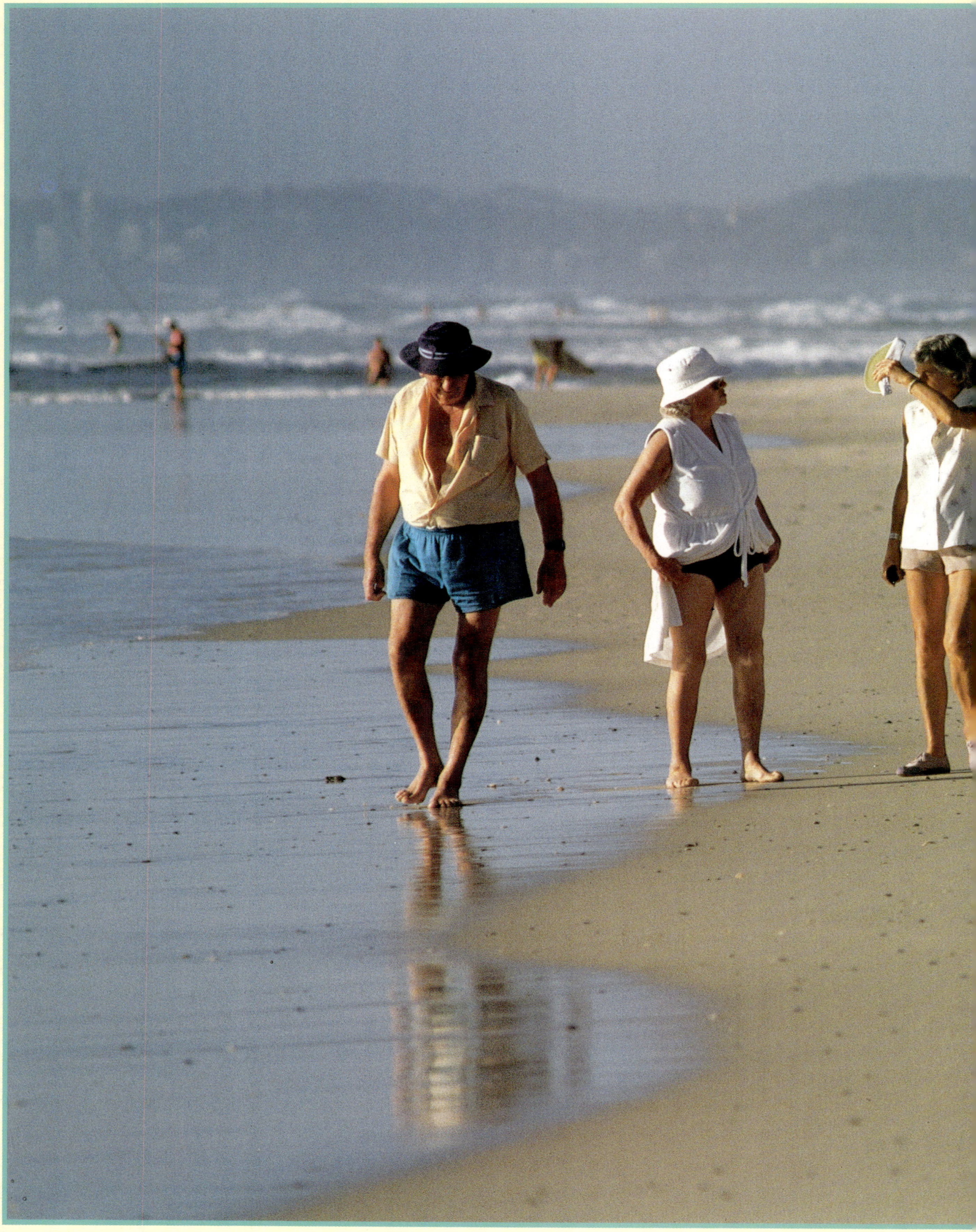

CHAPTER SIX

FITNESS FROM 8 TO 80

YOU ARE ONLY
AS OLD AS YOU FEEL!
REGULAR EXERCISE WILL
LEAD TO A FIT BODY
AND A FIT MIND

FITNESS FOR WOMEN

From early childhood participation in sports and development of fitness is expected of males in our society. These same expectations are often not placed on women. In the past, young women were discouraged from physical activity. Many Australian schools fostered this negative attitude; some even used activity, particularly running, as a punishment for misdemeanours. Although exercise is now actively encouraged in most schools, many women still enter their twenties with negative attitudes towards exercise and fitness.

Consequently it requires a greater effort for women to strive for fitness, but that effort is within the capacity of us all. Health and fitness need not be restricted to a fortunate few. It is necessary for women to realise that fitness is just as important and accessible to them as it is to males. Those who do are well aware of the health benefits, joy and exhilaration that an active lifestyle can bring. Fitness is a great confidence builder, it develops self-esteem and helps to relieve stress. A fit person not only looks and feels better, they have the glowing good health and vitality that accompanies a high quality lifestyle.

Although the human body is built for activity, our modern way of life fosters unfitness and below average health status. Our bodies have simply not kept pace with the rapid changes technology has forced upon us. We are surrounded by an ever increasing array of machines, which reduce the effort needed to perform even the most menial tasks. Food technology has developed a multitude of techniques for processing food with little or no nutritional value. Our day to day activities are no longer sufficient to maintain the body in a state of optimum health. To avoid ill health it is necessary for us to take steps to remedy this situation.

Exercising in a group helps to offset possible boredom.

WHAT IS FITNESS?

Fitness is more than just the absence of disease. It is the general ability of the heart, lungs, muscles, blood vessels and bones to function with optimum efficiency. In a sporting context, specific fitness is dictated by the needs of the particular sport. The fitness components required by a gymnast, marathon runner and weightlifter are quite different. Fitness therefore does not indicate who can run the fastest or the greatest distance or who is the strongest. It allows

A healthy lifestyle is important for the whole family.

you to perform daily tasks and to participate in recreational activities with pleasure and without fatigue.

There are four basic components of fitness for health:

Aerobic Fitness This is generally considered to be the most important component of fitness because it reduces the risk to our health from coronary heart disease. Aerobic fitness refers to the ability of the heart, lungs and blood vessels to deliver oxygen to the muscles and is sometimes called cardiovascular fitness or endurance. It helps to retard the deterioration of our physical capacity as we age and so contributes significantly to an improved quality of life. The decreased stress levels and positive self-image associated with aerobic fitness make a strong argument for us to achieve and maintain some degree of aerobic fitness for life.

Flexibility This refers to the ability to move a joint through its maximum range of motion. It depends on the ability of the muscles involved in the movement to stretch to their optimum length. Flexibility is needed for all sports as well as many everyday tasks.

Strength This is the ability of a muscle or muscle group to exert a maximum force against a resistance. It is probably the best known of the fitness components.

Strength is a basic requirement for almost all sports and is important in many daily activities.

Muscular Endurance

This refers to the ability of a muscle or muscle group to contract repeatedly, for example, when painting, performing sit-ups, or washing windows. It is often confused with strength. Although strength is required for muscular endurance, it refers to a maximum contraction, while endurance refers to repeated contractions.

There are a number of other components of fitness. Those who wish to extend their fitness for a particular sport may need to develop speed, power, agility, balance, co-ordination and motor skills.

WHY EXERCISE REGULARLY?

There are many reasons for including exercise in your lifestyle apart from the health and fitness benefits already mentioned. Physical activity is enjoyable and fun, especially if you choose to exercise with others in a pleasant social setting. You will discover that regular vigorous exercise actually increases rather than depletes your energy levels. This enables you to breeze through your day without fatigue. Consequently you will have more stamina at school, home or work.

To achieve the maximum benefit you need to exercise regularly. You should aim to exercise at least 3 times per week (4 or 5 is better) for between 30 and 60 minutes. Twice weekly, no matter how intensive or how long, simply does not have the same result. Neither will five 15 minute sessions. This is because short duration exercises burn the body's glucose. To burn fats you need long duration exercises. Fat tissue is stored energy — the longer you exercise, the greater chance you have of losing fat.

So if you want to get fit, get moving. Overweight people sometimes consume fewer kilojoules than thin people without losing weight because they are less active physically. The fitter you are, the greater the ability of your body to burn fats for energy. As well as producing a more efficient use of kilojoules from the food you eat, lean muscle tissue improves the absorption of nutrients. Exercise also speeds up your metabolic rate and improves your body circulation. It increases the efficiency of your cardiovascular system and reduces the risk of coronary heart disease.

As the appearance of your body changes through exercise, your self-esteem, confidence and vitality will be enhanced. You will experience an improved self-image and a more positive attitude to life. There is a significant retardation of the body's ageing process. You will have healthier skin with fewer wrinkles. People who exercise consume fewer drugs, less coffee, tea, alcohol, refined carbohydrates and sugar and are less prone to stress than sedentary people. Exercise promotes better sleeping habits and produces a more restful sleep.

Regular exercise improves your overall quality of life and leads to a fit body and a fit mind.

Fitness from 8 to 80

'Children don't run because it is a sensible way to stay healthy and fit — children run because it is fun!'

'Woman does not cease to play because she grows old, woman grows old because she ceases to play.'

with apologies to
GEORGE BERNARD SHAW.

HOW DO YOU START?

Once you have decided to pursue fitness and health it is unwise to jump in without a plan. A planned approach is a more effective way of achieving your goals and helps you to stick with it.

First you will need to assess your current health level. Many people wonder whether they need a medical clearance from their doctor before commencing an exercise program. You can determine this yourself by completing the Physical Activity Readiness Questionnaire (PAR-Q) on page 158. It is very simple. Read it carefully, answer the questions and follow the advice suggested.

HOW FIT ARE YOU?

Once you are cleared for activity you need to evaluate your present fitness levels. To do this you assess the components of fitness plus your body composition. A brief explanation of these tests is presented below. There are three options available — you can administer the tests at home yourself, you can be assessed by a qualified gym instructor, or, if you have access to a tertiary institution with a Human Movement department, they can advise you where such tests can be performed.

The four areas to be tested are as follows:

Body Composition Sometimes called the 'pinch test', this assesses the amount of fat which is deposited beneath the skin. The test is performed with skinfold calipers which measure the width of a skinfold at 8 specific body sites. The sum of these 8 measurements is calculated.

65

Aerobic Fitness This can be tested in several ways. The most accurate is a test of maximum oxygen consumption or VO_2 max. An estimation of this can be made from a test using an exercise bicycle, a step test, or a 12-minute run, swim or cycle test.

Abdominal Strength This involves a simple test using sit-ups. It can easily be performed at home.

Flexibility This is assessed by a sit and reach test. The equipment for this can be constructed.

See pages 162–168 for a detailed explanation of each test and a list of the tertiary institutions where advice can be obtained. You can test yourself at regular intervals to monitor your progress and keep you motivated to continue your exercise program. Every 6 to 10 weeks should be sufficient. Keep a record of all your results.

RECORD YOUR FITNESS

Three results sheets are included on pages 159–161. A completed example sheet is provided for each. Photocopy the pages and keep them in a binder as a record of your activity program and progress.

Training Log It is a good idea to fill out your activities a week in advance. (Do this in conjunction with your weekly time management plan.) Include alternatives in case the weather interferes. By planning your activities around your exercise you are more likely to stick to them than if you try and fit exercise into an already crowded schedule.

Fitness Test Results These will monitor your steady improvements and provide the essential motivation to keep going.

Swimming develops cardiovascular fitness and health.

FITNESS FROM 8 TO 80

Weight and Skinfold Chart Most people who embark on an exercise program are discouraged if they do not see a marked change in their weight immediately. A much more useful measure is the relation between your skinfold sum and your weight.

FOR THE OVER 35s

A lot of women wonder whether it is too late to get fit after age 35, or age 45, or age 55 and so on. The answer is simple. It is never too late.

Women over 60 can improve their aerobic fitness by as much as 50% through training (as measured by VO_2 max). In fact, what were once perceived as 'normal symptoms of ageing' are often only symptoms of inactivity.

It is thought that we can lose up to 10% of our aerobic capacity every 10 years after age 30. This is not necessarily the case for those who have remained physically active throughout their lives. An older woman can have an aerobic power comparable with many who are much younger. So while we cannot reverse the ageing process, we can slow it down considerably by adopting an active lifestyle which incorporates a healthy diet.

If you are in the older age bracket and have not been active for some years, then your program will need to be a little different from someone in her teens or twenties. Years of inactivity slow your speed and make you less flexible. Consequently exercise will be harder on your joints than it was when you were younger. You will simply need to program at a lower intensity and allow a longer recovery time than a younger person. Although your progress will be a little slower, with patience and perseverance you will still find the rewards worth the effort.

A medical examination is more urgent for those who plan to remain inactive than for those who intend to get into good physical shape.

Good habits that are begun early show themselves as you age. Don't be obsessed with getting rid of wrinkles. Look after your skin, but accept natural laughter lines as part of ageing.

You really are only as old as you feel. Start an exercise program and you will soon experience the joys of fitness, and have fun at the same time. When learning something new the challenge doesn't lie in your arms and legs, but in your head. Believe that you can achieve anything you want to. Exercise will help you re-examine what being old means for you.

CHILD'S PLAY

Children look up to adults. It is a great responsibility to show them that a healthy lifestyle, a fun fitness program, a balanced nutritional diet and time for leisure and relaxation are the ingredients to a full life.

To allow children to develop to their full potential they should be shown a variety of activities. When they are old enough to make their own decisions, hopefully they will choose a way of life that is healthy and beneficial.

Physical activity should be encouraged at a young age. However, if the attitude is to win at all costs, no competition is ever going to be fun. There are many more things children can learn from exercise other than just winning. These include being part of a team, respecting others for their ability, learning from their mistakes, acquiring new skills, establishing good habits from an early age, applying correct instruction of technique, learning discipline and self-motivation, improving self-image and self-responsibility, and participating in decision making.

There are a number of ways adults can assist children to get the most out of exercise. Encourage your children to play, it's a natural form of exercise. Dress your children appropriately for play and don't put unnecessary restrictions on them about getting their clothes dirty. Be careful not to push children. Childhood is short, and pushing them may destroy their motivation. Never compare your child with another of the same age; growth rate differences make this unrealistic. Teach children the safety aspects of exercise.

Include children in your exercise. Take them to the park and let them skate, bike, or kick a soccer ball as you run. Take active holidays and include some form of physical activity in your leisure time. Above all, be an example to them.

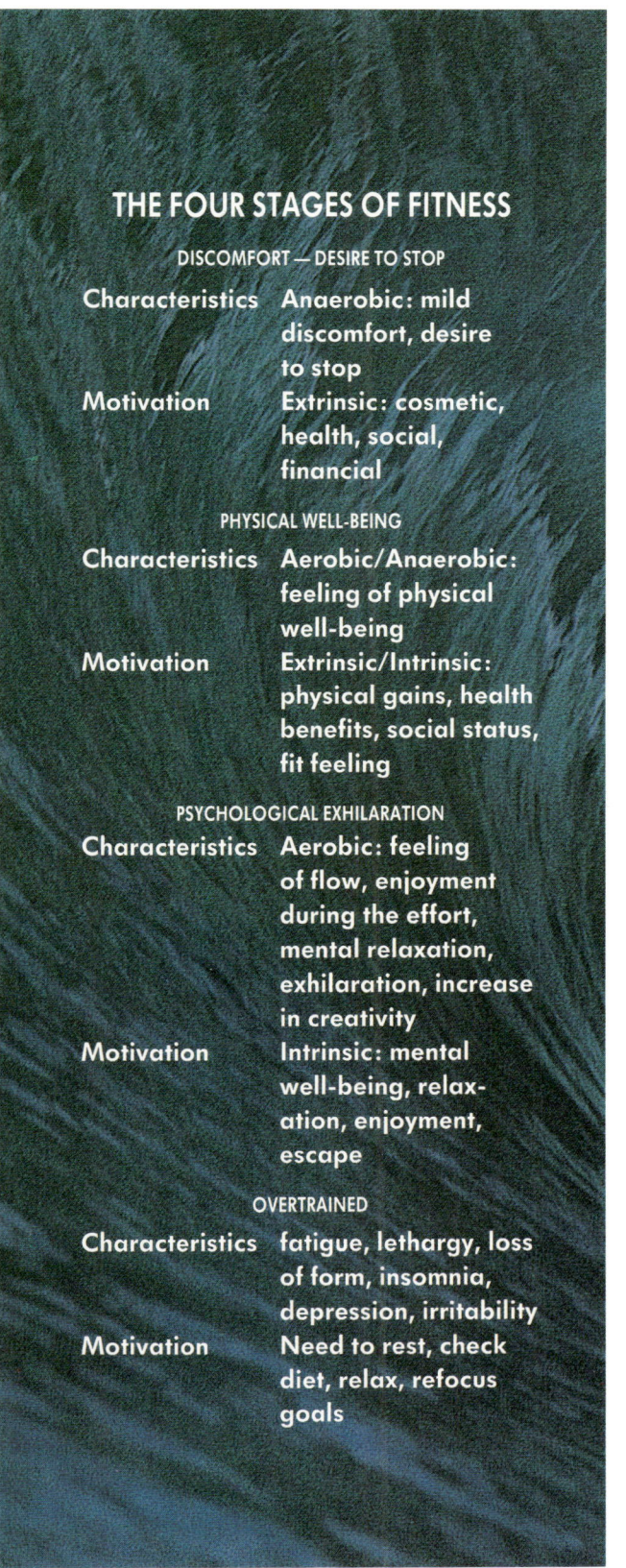

THE FOUR STAGES OF FITNESS

DISCOMFORT — DESIRE TO STOP
Characteristics Anaerobic: mild discomfort, desire to stop
Motivation Extrinsic: cosmetic, health, social, financial

PHYSICAL WELL-BEING
Characteristics Aerobic/Anaerobic: feeling of physical well-being
Motivation Extrinsic/Intrinsic: physical gains, health benefits, social status, fit feeling

PSYCHOLOGICAL EXHILARATION
Characteristics Aerobic: feeling of flow, enjoyment during the effort, mental relaxation, exhilaration, increase in creativity
Motivation Intrinsic: mental well-being, relaxation, enjoyment, escape

OVERTRAINED
Characteristics fatigue, lethargy, loss of form, insomnia, depression, irritability
Motivation Need to rest, check diet, relax, refocus goals

BODY TYPE

Determining your body type can help you set your fitness goals and choose which exercises are best suited to you. Whatever their age, each person can be categorised into one of three basic body types. These are classified according to a combination of skeleton size, body fat, height, weight and muscles. The appearance of your body type may be deceptive. As you change your exercise level and eating habits your body type will also change. The three dominant body types are endomorphic, mesomorphic and ectomorphic.

> **H**ere are some positive effects of an active lifestyle that reduce the 'normal symptoms of ageing'.
> - increased aerobic power
> - increased strength
> - increased flexibility
> - decreased fragility of bones that leads to osteoporosis
> - decreased weight that leads to obesity
> - decreased risk factors of coronary heart disease
> - increased quality of life

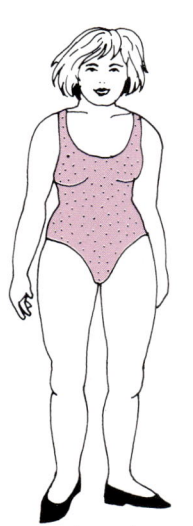

Endomorphic

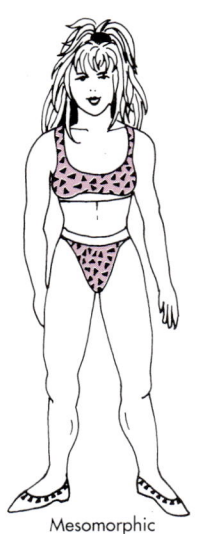

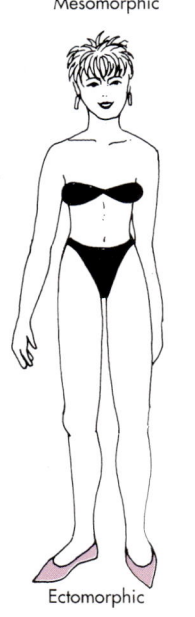

Mesomorphic

Ectomorphic

Endomorph This type has a large skeletal frame with a high percentage of body fat. The weight is concentrated in the area of the lower body, centred around the hips, waist, thighs and buttocks. The body is characterised by little muscle tone and rounded contours. With weight training and fitness, muscle definition emerges and body fat is lost. The body would then be classified as more mesomorphic. Low impact activities such as brisk walking, stationary cycling, swimming and low impact aerobics are best suited to this body type.

Mesomorph This type has a medium to large skeletal frame with a low level of body fat. The strong, firm body is of sturdy build and has a high level of muscular development. Most of the weight is concentrated in the upper body area rather than near the middle. Those with this body type can perform activities such as weight training, skiing, tennis and gymnastics.

Ectomorph This type has a light, lean skeletal frame with a low percentage of body fat. The body is tall and slender with a low level of muscularity. Endurance activities such as marathon running and aerobic dance are best suited to this body type.

Fitness from 8 to 80

CHILDREN	TEENAGERS	YOUNG ADULTS (20–39)	MIDDLE ADULTS (40–59)	SENIORS (60 OR OLDER)
Vigorous playtime 1 to 2 hours daily.	1 to 2 hours of sports or fitness activity 3 to 5 times a week.	½ to 1 hour vigorous aerobic activity 3 to 5 times per week.	½ to 1 hour aerobic activity 3 to 5 times a week.	Consult a doctor before beginning any new exercise program.
Join active neighbourhood play like riding bikes.	Go on active family vacations.	Learn warm up and cool-down stretches (or yoga). Do them 5 to 7 minutes each time before and after exercise.	Increase duration, reduce intensity to avoid injury.	½ to 1 hour moderate activity 3 times per week.
Go on family walks and short hikes.	Control weight gain with aerobic activities like walking, biking, jogging, or swimming.		Increase stretching before and after exercise (5 to 7 minutes minimum).	Concentrate on low-impact exercise.
Wear well-cushioned, flexible shoes.	Walk and talk with friends.	Take active vacations, hike, bike, swim, ski, row.	Use physical activity for stress management.	Learn a new sport like golf, tennis, ballroom dancing.
Join organised sports or dance programs.	Pursue sports that can be enjoyed for life: tennis, swimming, walking.	Put walking into your daily routine by walking to work (or part way to work) or on your lunch hour.	Reduce saturated fat and salt in your food.	Plan a daily walk that lasts at least 20 minutes.
	Join team sports.	Find exercise partners.	Concentrate on low-impact activity like walking, biking, swimming.	Enlist friends for walking and other exercises.
			Participate in social sports like tennis or golf.	

Reproduced courtesy of *The Walking Magazine*

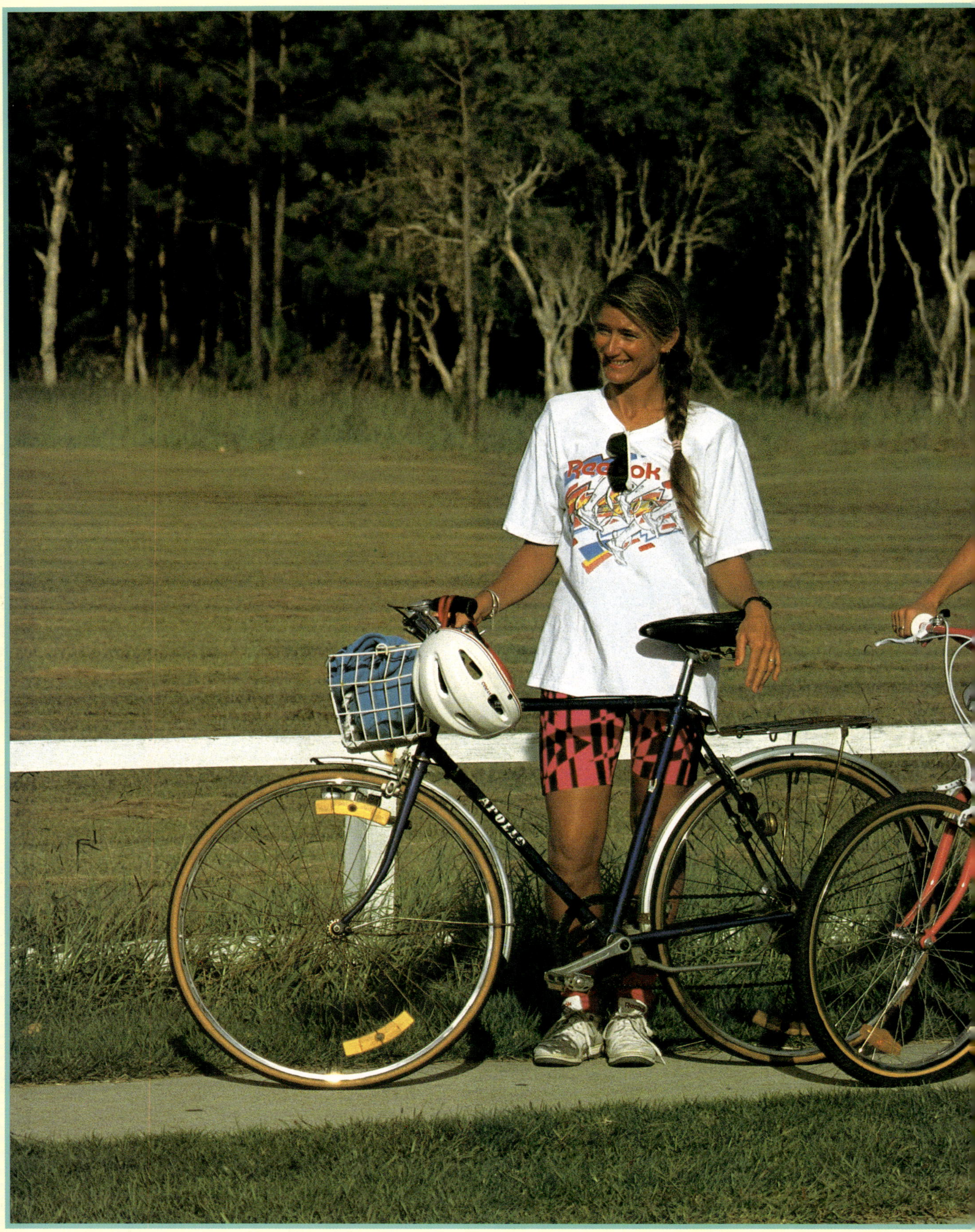
APOLLO

CHAPTER SEVEN
DESIGNING YOUR FITNESS PROGRAM

THE MOST IMPORTANT CONSIDERATION WHEN DESIGNING AN EXERCISE PROGRAM IS THAT YOU CHOOSE ACTIVITIES YOU ENJOY

FROM F.I.T. TO FITNESS

Choosing enjoyable exercises will enable you to incorporate the activities into your lifestyle and so maintain your program over time. Whatever activities you choose, it is a good idea to understand the basic principles of aerobic exercise programming.

To achieve the maximum health and weight control benefits you should follow the F.I.T. principle:

F is for frequency This refers to how often you should exercise. The minimum number is three times per week. This should be your starting point. Your long-term goal would then be to extend this to a daily activity period. Don't overdo exercise to begin with as injury or excessive discomfort can occur and this will dampen your spirits.

If you exercise 5 or 6 days per week, you need to be aware of the hard–easy principle. That is, if you do a hard workout on a given day, then the next day you need to follow up with an easy workout. Some small muscle fibres are inevitably damaged during a hard workout and this gives them time to heal. Two back-to-back hard sessions will increase the damage and prolong repair time. This results in discomfort, stiffness and muscle soreness.

I is for intensity This refers to how hard you should exercise to obtain a required effect. Your current level of fitness will determine where you start and where you set your targets for each session. This is based on your training heart rate (THR). You will need to become proficient at taking your heart rate during exercise, as shown in the accompanying photographs.

To take your pulse use your first two fingers (not your thumb). Press lightly on your radial artery, close to your thumb on the inside of your wrist, or on your carotid artery, straight down from the corner of your eye, just under your chin. Count the number of beats for 10 seconds and multiply by six.

Monitor your heart rate during exercise by taking your pulse frequently.

To calculate your training heart rate (THR):

First, measure your resting heart rate (RHR). The best time to do this is first thing in the morning.

Secondly, calculate your maximum heart rate (MHR). To do this you simply subtract your age from 220. Therefore a 40-year-old woman would have a maximum heart rate of 180 beats per minute (ie, 220 − 40 = 180).

Thirdly, determine your exercise intensity according to the following ranges:

Getting Started:	60–70%
Getting Better:	70–80%
Keeping it Going:	80–90%

To calculate your training heart range (THR) use the following formula:

THR = ...% × (MHR — RHR) + RHR

Here is an example for a 40-year-old beginner with a resting heart rate of 70.

$$\begin{aligned} THR &= 0.60 \times (180-70) + 70 \\ &\text{(60\% is equivalent to 0.60)} \\ &= 0.60 \times 110 + 70 \\ &= 66 + 70 \\ &= 136 \end{aligned}$$

The following graph illustrates the training zone for all age groups based on a resting heart rate of 70. The 60% line represents the lower limit for those starting out, while the 90% line is for those competing at an elite level in a sport.

Designing your Fitness Program

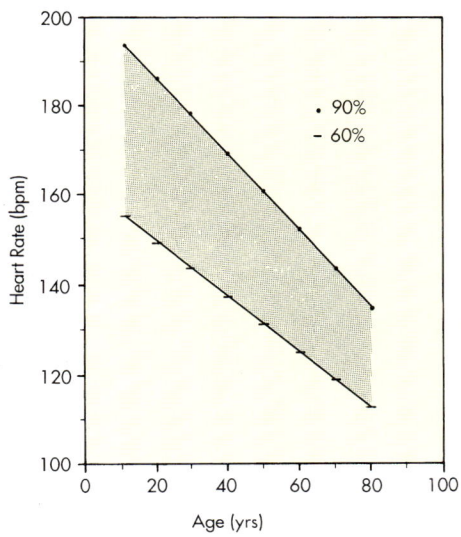

Start at the lower limit for your fitness group (i.e. 60% for someone **Getting Started,** 70% for someone **Getting Better** etc.) and gradually increase the percentage as your fitness improves. Proceed slowly. Don't be in too much hurry to get to the next level.

During exercise take your heart rate at convenient intervals (every 10 minutes is suitable) to ensure you are keeping close to your target and that your exercise heart rate is within your training zone. If you wish, you can purchase products that will monitor your heart rate throughout your workout.

This formula is a general guide to determine your heart rate. It is important to also listen to your body for signs of over-exertion,

A dip in the ocean is an invigorating finish to a jog along the beach.

such as pounding in your chest, dizziness, faintness or profuse sweating. Cool down for 5 to 10 minutes before ending your workout. See your doctor if these symptoms persist.

T is for time This refers to how long you should exercise. Generally, this should be at least 15–20 minutes for there to be any health and weight control benefits, preferably longer for significant benefit. Aim to progress to a minimum of 30 minutes of continuous, rhythmic exercise. A duration of 45 minutes or more is better for weight control. In order to do this you will need to decrease your intensity. This is particularly important for those in a low fitness category and those who are overweight.

FITNESS

In order to improve you must continually progress by gradual increases in either of the three F.I.T. factors. You can increase one of the following while keeping the other two factors the same:

FREQUENCY	from 3 up to 7 times per week or
INTENSITY	from 60% up to 90% or
TIME	from 30 minutes onwards

There are many different combinations. They can be tailored to suit your own needs, interests and time available. Never increase your weekly training volume by more than 10%.

The following sections detail six aerobic activities. These have been chosen because they are continuous and will enable you to maintain your training heart rate. They should form the central part or core of your program. They are called 'aerobic' because they require an on-going supply of oxygen to maintain the activity. During these activities, oxygen is required at a much faster rate than under resting conditions. The cardiovascular system becomes overloaded and must therefore 'train' itself to handle the situation more efficiently. Other activities such as tennis, squash and netball are intermittent and your heart rate fluctuates with the changing intensity of the exercise. While they are good in their own right as a means of burning extra kilojoules, these intermittent activities should be seen as additions to your core program.

When you design your own aerobic program, every workout should have three phases irrespective of the activity chosen. They are:

WARM UP — STRETCHING

CONDITIONING ACTIVITY — CONTINUOUS AEROBIC EXERCISE

COOL DOWN — STRETCHING

WARM UP

As the name suggests, this is designed to increase the body's internal temperature. This in turn stimulates the heart and lungs to increase heart rate and breathing rate to prepare for the prolonged activity session. It also warms up the muscles by increasing their blood flow. This allows muscles and tendons to be more flexible, decreases the chance of strains or sprains, and thereby reduces the stiffness we often feel after a strenuous exercise session.

The time required for warm up will vary from person to person. Older women, and particularly those who have not been active for some time will need to warm up for a longer period, as will those who are exercising in cold weather.

Take your time in a stretching routine. Get to know your own limits. There is no competition involved, everyone's stretching capabilities are different. Don't overstretch. Any strain, pain or shaking of muscles could cause injury.

DESIGNING YOUR FITNESS PROGRAM

There are a few general points to remember when stretching:

1 Keep your head in a neutral position with the ears over the shoulders as shown:

standing   lying   on hands and knees

2 Always fix your eyes on a position straight ahead.
3 Check your posture at all times. Chest lifted out, shoulders back, tummy in.
4 Breathe evenly. Do not hold your breath. Inhale through the nose and as you exhale, relax deeper into the stretch.

There are an endless number of body stretches to do for all sorts of activities. The following photographs show stretches that progress from the upper to lower body. You should add other stretches depending on your chosen activity. It should take about 10 minutes to complete the set. Hold each stretch for between 10 and 20 seconds, longer if you wish. Feel the stretch and concentrate on the muscles being stretched.

F. I. T.

FREQUENCY
three times per week is the minimum for significant gains in fitness levels

INTENSITY
calculate your training heart zone and work within this level as much as possible

TIME
your workout should be a minimum of 30 minutes in duration

NECK
- hold stretching side arm behind back
- look straight ahead
- gently lower head to side until mildly tight on neck

TRUNK
- stomach in, shoulders back
- knees slightly bent, feet shoulder width apart, fingers forward, reach high

77

LISA CURRY'S TOTAL HEALTH & FITNESS

SHOULDERS
- back straight
- knees slightly bent, feet shoulder width apart
- clasp hands
- gently push arms up and backward until mild tightness in shoulder

BACK OF UPPER ARM
- back straight
- knees slightly bent, feet shoulder width apart
- gently push elbow down
- palm of hand flat on vertebrae of neck

LOWER BACK
- head on floor, bend knees, gently pull knees to chest
- back straight. look ahead. Focus on object, hands around upper leg, gently pull to chest

78

Back of Thigh
- head on floor, lower leg — foot on floor
- upper leg — bend knee, gently straighten until mild tightness

Chest
- back straight
- knees slightly bent, feet shoulder width apart
- shoulders back, stomach in
- clasp hands behind
- gently push arms up until mild tightness in chest

Lower Back
- back straight, look ahead.
- focus on object
- hands around upper leg, gently pull to chest

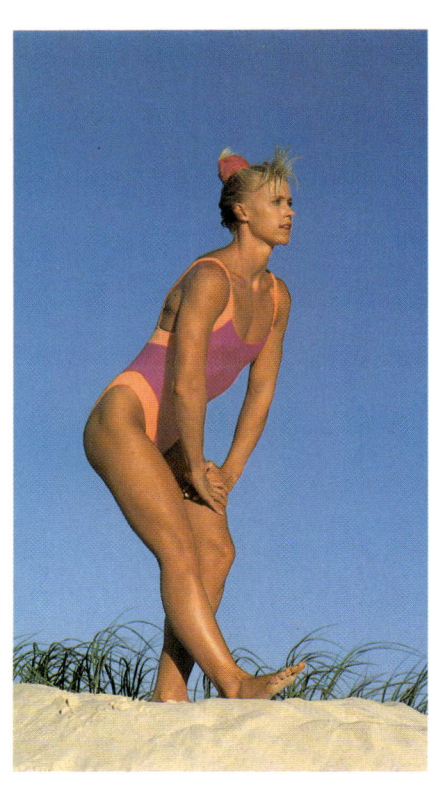

BACK OF THIGH
- back leg bent
- lean slightly forward
- eyes ahead
- support arms
- front leg straight toe raised
- gently pull buttocks backwards until mild tightness on back of thigh

FRONT OF THIGH
- hold onto sturdy support and focus on object
- straight posture
- lift leg by ankle
- ensure knees together

NB For more complete stretch, use opposite hand to foot

FRONT OF THIGH
- chin down, knees together
- with same side hand as foot, gently pull ankle back until mild tightness in front thigh

NB If knee hurts, stop. Use towel around foot if you cannot reach.

DESIGNING YOUR FITNESS PROGRAM

CALF
- look at floor
- back straight
- front leg — thigh vertical
- back leg straight and gently lower heel to floor until mildly tight on calf

CALF
- straight back
- eyes forward
- toes forward
- front foot directly below knee
- keep back heel on floor
- slowly bend knees until mild tightness in back leg calf

LISTEN TO YOUR BODY

If you have aching muscles or fever associated with the flu, stop exercising. Recuperate, relax and drink lots of water. When you are feeling better, steadily pace yourself back into your exercise routine.

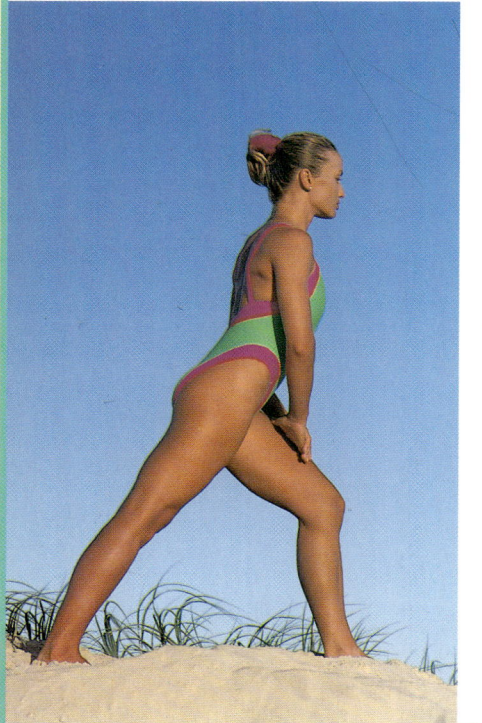

HIPS
- front foot in front of knee
- opposite hand support on floor
- back foot — toes pointing forward
- relax hip towards floor

HIPS
- back straight
- stomach in
- eyes forward
- hips square to front
- all toes forward
- back leg straight
- gently lean forward

CONDITIONING ACTIVITY

This should occupy the longest time in your workout, a minimum of 20–30 minutes. The time is determined by your current level of fitness. How you organise this is entirely up to you. You may want to participate in a single activity such as running, or you may want to design a combination program of running, cycling and swimming. There is no one 'right' activity.

Choosing several different activities, called cross-training, is a good way of retaining your motivation, particularly if all activities are easily accessible. The advantage in choosing a single activity is that you will progress more rapidly. The risk of boredom can be offset by exercising with others, which also helps to sustain motivation.

The plan you design has an infinite number of

Designing your Fitness Program

variations. Feel free to experiment with as many variations as you like. The only limitation is that it conforms to the F.I.T. principle:

FREQUENCY   at least 3 times per week

INTENSITY   at an intensity that will produce a training effect

TIME   for at least 30 minutes each workout

Cool Down

Following your conditioning activity, it is wise to allow a further period of approximately five minutes to taper off and allow your body to cool down gradually. This slows down blood flow and helps prevent a sudden drop in blood pressure.

Start the cool down with a continuation of the conditioning activity, but at a much lower intensity (to bring your heart rate down below 100 beats per minute) and finish off with the stretches. Stretching exercises performed at this time helps reduce the muscle soreness that often occurs on the day following a workout.

The following sections on each activity have been written with the same section headings so that you can compare them easily and determine which activity suits you best. Each section lists:

BENEFITS
MUSCLES WORKED
KILOJOULES EXPENDED
(E.G. WALK IT OFF)
EQUIPMENT
EXTRA STRETCHES
TECHNIQUE
DESIGNING A PROGRAM
TAKING IT FURTHER

The focus of each section is on designing a program. The programs suggested are in three levels. **Getting Started** is for those who are just beginning an exercise program or for those who have been inactive for many years; the second level **Getting Better** is for those who already have some degree of fitness and who have been relatively active; the third level **Keeping it Going** is designed to equip you for a high level of fitness and perhaps for competition if you wish. Note that your level may vary from activity to activity. For example, you might be at the third level in running, but, because of lack of experience, at the **Getting Started** level of swimming.

The chart below tells you how the benefits of the six activities compare:

ACTIVITY	AEROBIC FITNESS	STRENGTH	FLEXIBILITY	MUSCULAR ENDURANCE	WEIGHT CONTROL
WALKING	★★★	★	★	★★	★★★
RUNNING	★★★★	★	★	★★★	★★★★
SWIMMING	★★★★	★★	★★	★★★	★★★
CYCLING	★★★★	★★	★	★★★	★★★
AEROBIC DANCE	★★★	★★	★★★	★★★	★★★
WEIGHT TRAINING	★	★★★★	★	★★★	★★

KEY   ★★★★ excellent   ★★★ good   ★★ fair   ★ poor

WALKING

BENEFITS

Not only is walking an exercise for everyone, it is the exercise our bodies were designed for. A walking program provides a good aerobic workout with fitness and health benefits, provided the F. I. T. principles are followed. Walking does not place a heavy strain on the ligaments and tendons of the joints of the hip and leg. You can therefore expect to exercise free from injury.

Walking should be the mode of exercise for those **Getting Started**, particularly for older women who have not exercised for some time and those who are overweight.

There will be many people who want to exercise for health benefits, but who just do not want to run. You may progress to a running program later, but don't be in a hurry to move on. Doing too much too soon can lead to injury, frustration, loss of interest and dropping out.

There are many different ways

of making your walking program interesting and beneficial. By walking with a group of friends you can make your workout a fun, social occasion. You can involve your whole family and incorporate hiking trips into your program. If walking by yourself, you can use headphones, or just enjoy the solitude.

Muscles Worked

Walking uses almost all of the body's 206 bones and 660 muscles. It is excellent for the major muscles of the upper and lower legs as well as the buttocks. Walking with water weights will contribute to your upper muscular (including postural and spinal muscles) and whole body workout.

Walk It Off!

ACTIVITY LEVEL	KILOJOULES (CALORIES) PER 30 MINUTES
4 km/hr	397 (95)
7 km/hr	753 (180)
10 km/hr	1268 (303)

Equipment

Shoes Wearing shoes is essential for support and comfort. They should have a fairly flexible forefoot, straight padded, without too much inward curve. For pacewalking they may need to be half a size bigger, because of the forefoot movement.

Clothing The choice of clothing depends very much on climate. Whatever the weather the choice should be something that is loose-fitting and comfortable. Tight-fitting clothes restrict movement and can cause chaffing. Clothes should be light and cotton to allow heat dissipation. In cooler weather wear several layers that can be removed as your body warms up. As a general rule wear as little as you need.

Socks These should not be 100% cotton as the moisture from perspiring feet will remain in the sock causing rubbing. Choose a cotton/nylon or wool/nylon mix with a good stitched heel.

Hats In summer hats provide extra protection (with sunscreen) for the face from the strong rays of the sun. As with clothing, it is important to allow air to circulate freely and cool the head. In cold weather a hat will prevent you losing too much body heat via the head. Hats also protect you from the rain.

Sunglasses These will help protect your eyes from glare.

Gloves They can be worn in cold weather to protect the hands.

Backpacks Look for a pack that suits your needs. There is no cause to carry a large pack if you have only a few items. Choose a pack with easily accessible zippered pockets. Nylon is preferable because it is light, strong and water resistant. Carrying smaller packs around the waist is also popular, especially when pacewalking.

Fluids During summer avoid the hottest part of the day. Walk in the morning or early evening. You need to replace fluids lost in sweat by drinking every 15–20 minutes. Carrying walking water weights (even half full) will help alleviate your dehydration problems in hot weather.

EXTRA STRETCHES
Whole body stretches.

TECHNIQUE
When walking casually, shoulders are relaxed. Be careful to maintain this relaxed, upright posture and keep the spine erect. Look at the pavement immediately in front by casting your eyes downward rather than by bending your neck. Keep hips loose. Rolling from side to side is okay.

Your footstrike should be firstly on the outside corner of the heel, then roll forward along the outer edge of your foot, pushing off with all your toes at the same time. Do not curl up the toes as this will cramp them.

Designing your Fitness Program

and look ahead. Bending over and looking at the ground will cause you to shorten your stride, and fatigue and back pain will follow. Your arms should swing freely, don't clench your fists. Find a stride length and speed that are comfortable for you, and will take you to your training zone.

Utilise air more efficently by breathing rhythmically. Link your breathing with your gait, e.g. breathe in for 2 paces and out for 2 paces. Breathe air down towards the stomach. Move your abdomen out as speed and rate of breathing increases. If you get 'stitch' (cramping of the diaphragm), obtain the quickest relief by pressing hard with three fingers on the point where the pain is concentrated, usually just under the rib cage, while exhaling forcefully. Do this while continuing to walk.

BRISK WALKING

For brisk walking, posture is important. Keep shoulders back

PACEWALKING

As your fitness improves, increase your speed and stride length so that you are pacewalking (sometimes called 'power walking'), rather than walking briskly. This can be accomplished by improving the strength of your take-off phase, as your foot leaves the ground. Your arm motion should be more energetic with a slightly bent elbow.

For pacewalking, lengthen your stride to increase performance, rather than using quicker, shorter steps. Keep knees slightly bent to avoid jarring the knees and lower back, particularly on the downhills. This ensures you give your quadricep muscles (thighs) a good workout. Shin soreness is the most common problem for pacewalkers due to the extra pressure on the Tibialis Anterior muscle. Prevent soreness by specific stretching before, after and even during the walk.

WALKING

87

WALKING

Use a pumping arm action for vigorous walking. The elbow is bent at 90° throughout the swing, and the hands are relaxed. The arm swing works with the body's natural rhythm to propel the opposite arm forward as the leg strides out. On the forward swing, the hand should reach a comfortable position at about chest height. On the backswing, stop when you feel the muscles on the back part of the shoulder begin to stretch.

Avoid swinging arms across the chest. This oblique motion hinders your forward momentum, particularly when carrying water weights. This twisting motion of the torso can also lead to injury of the lower back. Keep arms swinging generally front to back, not side to side. Avoid tension, muscle clenching and tightness of arms and shoulders.

On undulating and uneven terrain you need to change your technique. When walking uphill lean slightly forward, reach out with arms and take shorter strides. On a downhill walk, lean slightly back, bend knees, hug arms closer to the body and lengthen your stride slightly.

DESIGNING A PROGRAM

Fit the program into your day by getting up early and walking before breakfast. Walk to work if it is reasonably close or get off your bus a few stops earlier. Walk in your lunch break or go for a brisk walk around your local shopping centre.

	GETTING STARTED	GETTING BETTER	KEEPING IT GOING
START AT:	brisk walking (8 weeks)	striding (8 weeks)	pacewalking lifelong
F	3 × week	4 × week	5 × week
I	4 km/hr	4.5 km/hr	5.2 km/hr
T	15–20 mins	45 mins	60 mins
BUILD TO:			
F	4 × week	4 × week	6–7 × week
I	3.5–5 km/hr	5 km/hr	6.5–8 km/hr
T	45 mins	60 mins	70 mins

Remember that walking at a heart rate below your training zone will not provide the same health benefits that a higher intensity will, though it will have a positive effect on weight control if the duration is 40 minutes or longer.

Taking It Further

Pacewalkers can increase the intensity of their program in several ways, all of which can be accompanied by the use of hand-held water weights.

Surging You can use interval training to bolster strength and endurance. Two or three times during the walk, surge (giving all you've got) for 1 km at a time. This may be done on the flat or up hills.

> Pace walking can be sustained for a longer period of time than other high-energy activities like jogging. Fat deposits are therefore used by the body as its energy supply.

Striding Drop your centre of gravity, increase stride length as much as possible without jeopardising technique. 'Power' with arms to head height in front and shoulder height behind. Aim to travel approximately 100–150 metres.

Retro Action This is walking backwards. Putting the body in reverse is an effective method of rehabilitation from injury and training. Moving backwards moves joints in the opposite direction. The result is increased flexibility and muscle parity in the legs. You can also raise your heart rate more quickly, particularly walking backwards up a small incline. Technique is of course different. The ball of the foot contacts first, push off with heel, keep joints 'soft'. Swing arms comfortably in opposition to the legs, concentrating especially on push and lift behind. Look comfortably over one shoulder and watch for obstacles. Aim to travel approximately 100 metres.

Soft Sand This is an excellent heart rate boosting activity, which can strengthen ligaments from the lower back to the feet and increase energy expenditure by up to 50 per cent. Maintain correct pacewalking technique and try to walk 'into' the sand. The increased resistance in the surface causes the heart rate to elevate. Aim to continue for up to 1 km. Correct footwear is essential.

For all of the above, your training heart rate should be 75–80 per cent. All these activities may be incor-

> Walking 1 kilometre will yield the same kilojoule expenditure as running 1 kilometre, it just takes longer.

porated within a longer walk of 60–75 minutes. When surging, striding, retro or soft sand walking, pay special attention to long, even strides. Avoid small, jerky steps. Be aware of the signs of over-stressing your body — lingering soreness, heavy leggedness, apathy, high resting pulse, insomnia, appetite loss, irritability, headaches.

Race walking introduces a competitive aspect that some may find a challenging and rewarding goal. Technique, however, is quite different and specialist coaching is advisable.

DIFFERENCES IN FOOT STRIDE

STROLLING
Normal walking — arms swing freely at your side.

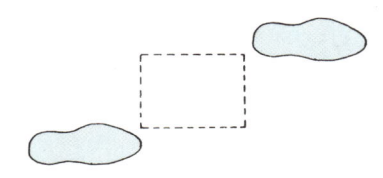

BRISK WALKING
Great for burning fat. Take long slow walks (40-60 minutes or more) at about 60% of your maximum heart rate, 5-7 times a week. Feel your body working. Increase your stride slightly and start to swing your arms in a controlled manner.

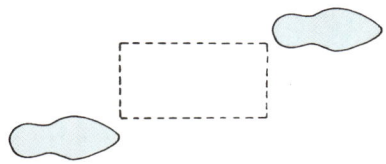

PACE WALKING
As you progress to pace walking your stride lengthens and your feet land closer to an imaginary centre line extending straight ahead of you. Pump with the arms. Include hills and soft sand if possible.

RACE WALKING
During race walking, both feet land on that imaginary line as a result of a dramatically rotating pelvis. Arms work across the body.

KAY PHILLIPS AND PACEWALKING
Kay Phillips is the founder and leader of the 'Waveside Walkers' from TriFitness Gym in Maroochydore, Queensland. She started her walking program after sustaining a lower back injury while teaching physical education. Constant daily jogging and high impact competitive sport also contributed to disc degeneration.
Walking was an enjoyable alternative for rehabilitation and has become Kay's lifetime commitment. Today she is the fearless leader of about 40 keen walkers who pace it out five times a week. Everyone can walk and learning the various stages can help you turn your walking into a lifelong fitness benefit.
Kay demonstrates the walks in this book.

A bunion, blister or ingrown toenail can give you back pain.
If you try to take the pressure off the painful area of your foot, you can throw your weight in the opposite direction. This will result in a changed walking gait. You will push muscles out of alignment and cause muscular fatigue and soreness.

RUNNING

BENEFITS

Running is a good activity to include in the core of your exercise program because it uses the large muscle groups of the legs and lower back, and it burns more kilojoules per unit of time than most other aerobic exercise. Running is convenient and accessible, has no difficult skills to learn and even sedentary people can show cardiovascular improvement very quickly.

The human body is designed for an endurance activity like running. Our upright posture, mode of movement, relatively hairless skin (and hence efficient cooling system) and diet all suit us for this activity. Our modern lifestyle has eliminated the need for us to perform endurance exercise, and this has led to an increase in the incidence of coronary heart disease and obesity, and to conditions like diabetes and hypertension (high blood pressure). The inclusion of running in your lifestyle can minimise the risk from all these conditions.

One of the principal benefits from running, particularly long slow distance running, is weight control. Obesity is a major factor in coronary heart disease, hypertension and diabetes. The maintenance of your ideal weight also boosts self-confidence and self-esteem.

Research has shown that runners have higher levels of HDLs

(High Density Lipoproteins) than their sedentary counterparts, which offers them more protection against coronary heart disease.

Muscles Worked

Calves, hamstrings, quadriceps and gluteus. Running also strengthens the lower back.

Run It Off!

ACTIVITY LEVEL	KILOJOULES (CALORIES) PER 30 MINUTES
9 km/hr	1205 (288)
10 km/hr	1318 (315)
12 km/hr	1620 (387)

Equipment

Very little equipment is required for a running program so the money saved should be put towards the purchase of your running shoes.

Shoes For every kilometre you run, each foot lands approximately 500 times. When you take your body weight into account you have a total impact of approximately 30 000 tonnes for each foot per kilometre. These impact forces are transmitted from your feet, through your ankles and hips to your spine. If you are not wearing a good shoe, your chance of injury to one or more of these joints is increased. Because people vary considerably in characteristics like height, weight, running style and choice of running surface, it doesn't necessarily follow that the most expensive shoe is the best. When making your purchase go to a reputable dealer, preferably one staffed by runners who will understand your individual needs. (See also page 169 'Hints on how to buy a running shoe')

Clothing You do not have to spend a lot of money on running attire, but an outfit that looks and feels good can have a positive effect on your persistence.

Dress for comfort according to the weather. Loose comfortable shorts and a t-shirt are ideal. Nylon shorts will keep chafing to a minimum and cotton-blend shirt and socks will improve comfort by absorbing moisture easily. Choose white or light colours as they reflect the heat and are easier to see at night than dark colours. Light mesh tops are excellent for the Australian summer time. In cold weather adopt a layered approach. Remove layers as your body warms up. Gloves and a woollen cap will also be useful.

Surfaces Once you have purchased shoes that suit your height, weight and running style you can run with reasonable safety on any surface. Grass is the preferred surface, provided it is even and firm, because of its 'giving' characteristics. However, it is not always possible for city dwellers to find suitable grassy surfaces. If you must run on either bitumen or concrete, choose bitumen as it has more 'give' than concrete.

If you run on the beach choose firmer sand where possible. Because sand does not have the same firmness as grass or concrete you will tire more quickly. Always wear your running shoes on sand.

When running on the road and on sand the camber or slope can put extra stress on the legs and knees. To avoid injury choose the flattest part of the beach or road.

EXTRA STRETCHES

As running uses the large muscles of the legs and lower back as well as the arms, a whole body stretch is recommended.

TECHNIQUE

An upright posture conserves your energy more efficiently. Run with your back comfortably straight, head up and shoulders relaxed. Leaning too far forward can lead to shin splints and lower back problems. Bend your arms with your hands in a comfortable position, not clenched tight. Minimise arm swing to maintain good balance. Don't overstride or understride as both are inefficient. Learn to 'float' over the ground.

Many beginners who run on the balls of their feet complain of leg problems. Practise running with the heel-to-toe technique. Land on the heel first with knees slightly bent, then transfer your weight to the ball of the foot by landing on the outer edge of your foot (called supination) and rolling inwards (called pronation).

To run uphill lean forward and pump with arms. To run downhill lean back and drop arms so they will swing lower.

DESIGNING A PROGRAM

	RUN / WALK		
	GETTING STARTED	GETTING BETTER	KEEPING IT GOING
START AT:			
F	3 × week	4 × week	5 × week
I	(run 1 min, walk 30 secs) × 10	(run 5 mins, walk 1 min) × 5	(run 10 mins walk 1 min) × 3
T	15 mins	30 mins	33 mins
BUILD TO:			
F	4 × week	5 × week	5 × week
I	(run 3 mins, walk 1 min) × 6	(run 10 mins, walk 2 mins) × 3	(run approx 4 km no walk)
T	24 mins	36 mins	30 mins

To take the run and walk program further: Include hills (run up, walk down). Run and walk on the beach, and have a refreshing swim afterwards.

DESIGNING YOUR FITNESS PROGRAM

RUN

	GETTING STARTED	GETTING BETTER	KEEPING IT GOING
START AT:			
F	3 × week	4 × week	5 × week
I	2–2.5 kms	6–6.5 kms	see below*
T	15 mins	35 mins	40 mins
BUILD TO:			
F	4 × week	4 × week	6 × week
I	approx 5 kms	7–7.5 kms	see below*
T	30 mins	40 mins	60 mins

*As the volume of your training increases it becomes important to adopt the hard–easy principle, i.e. a hard session one day, followed by an easy one the next day. The following example provides a possible model, but there are many other combinations that you can devise for yourself to suit your own situation. Don't increase your training volume by more than 10% per week.

	DISTANCE	INTENSITY
Monday	8–10 km	hard (80–85%)
Tuesday	5–6 km	easy (75%)
Wednesday	8–10 km	hard (80–85%)
Thursday	5–6 km	easy (75%)
Friday	8–10 km	hard (80–85%)
Saturday	Rest	
Sunday	12–15 km	easy (75%)

DIFFERENT PROGRAMS

Running forms the core of programs with different goals and consequently they are structured slightly differently. The following table gives a guide with the approximate F. I. T. factors for each type of program.

	WEIGHT CONTROL	HEALTH & FITNESS	ENDURANCE, SPORTS FITNESS
F	5–7 × week	3–5 × week	5–7 × week
I	40–60%	60–75%	75–85%
T	> 60 mins	20–40 mins	> 45 mins

TAKING IT FURTHER

There are various competitions available to the runner. You can participate in track athletics. If you wish to compete over short distances you will need to seek advice on a sprint program to supplement the aerobic program outlined. Longer distance runs — fun runs, half marathons and marathons — are conducted regularly throughout Australia. Veterans' competitions are also available in most capital cities with distances ranging from 100 metres to the marathon.

RUNNING

95

SWIMMING

BENEFITS

Swimming is a good exercise for development of cardiovascular fitness and health. It also improves flexibility and strength and contributes to whole-body toning.

Less stress is placed on the joints because of the buoyant effect of the water. This reduces the incidence of injury and muscle soreness encountered in many other activities. As a result swimming is ideal for those who have any form of physical impairment including arthritis, back problems, or joint disorders, and those who are overweight or recovering from injury.

The different swimming strokes use different muscle groups. Alternating the strokes enables you to get a whole body workout from the one activity, something no other single activity aerobic exercise can do to the same extent. Freestyle is the best stroke for the development of fitness. Other strokes add variety and reduce the boredom factor.

However, swimming has a specific skill aspect not associated with most other aerobic activities. An inefficient stroke will reduce the benefits of exercise. If you wish to include swimming in your program, but are not yet proficient, it is advisable to take some lessons before you start. Most pools have classes for a wide range of ages and ability levels.

Muscles Worked

Swimming is good for your arms, shoulders and chest. The inclusion of kick drills exercises your legs and buttocks.

Swim It Off!

Activity Level	Kilojoules (Calories) per 30 minutes
25m/mins	623 (149)
40m/mins	904 (216)
50m/mins	1297 (310)

Equipment

To swim for fitness and health with the appropriate intensity you need to swim in a pool that has lanes or markings on the bottom rather than the open waters of rivers or lakes. Most Australian public pools are 50 metres long with a few older ones measuring 55 yards. Some measure 25 metres (or 25 yards). The pace clock at the pool can be used to check your training heart rate to ensure that you are within your training zone.

Swimsuit Use a lycra or nylon fabric swimsuit. They are quick drying and comfortable.

Goggles These are worn to protect the eyes from the irritation of chlorine. They will also help you to see clearly. Make sure they fit tight and don't leak.

Cap These come in many shapes and sizes. Caps protect your hair and help keep it out of your eyes. If you have long hair, not wearing a cap can cause neck and shoulder ache.

Kickboard These will strengthen legs and improve your technique.

Pull-buoy These keep legs afloat to allow arm stroke to be strengthened.

Hand paddles These help improve stroke strength and technique by increasing resistance. This in turn strengthens your shoulders, arms and chest. Hand paddles with perforations reduce the strain on the shoulders and allow the hands to continually feel the water.

Extra Stretches

As most muscle groups are worked, use a whole body stretch.

Technique

Freestyle is the most efficient swimming stroke in terms of time and distance, and is consequently favoured by most people. An inefficient stroke uses excess energy by reducing the distance covered in a set time. Learning the correct technique will enhance your enjoyment and ensure that you train efficiently.

Keep the following points in mind for freestyle swimming:

Body position The body must be in a horizontal position along the surface of the water. Keep eyes looking forward slightly (about 45 degrees) and downward. The water around your face should be at your hairline.

Kick Kicking doesn't contribute much to speed through the water. The main function of a well-controlled kick is balance. It is important to kick consistently, whether it be a slow, medium or fast kick. Don't make big splashes; kick just under the surface so that you 'boil' the water. The timing of the kick depends on the length of your arm stroke, but may change according to your speed. People usually find a slower kick rate is best when swimming at a slow to moderate pace. As you pick up speed, for instance in a sprint, increase the rating of your kick. Kick from the hip, not just from the knee. The use of flippers can help strengthen your legs and buttocks as long as you put in enough effort.

Underwater stroke Stand waist deep in water and move each hand alternately through the water in a sideways 8 motion (i.e. ∞) with your hand flat and fingers slightly apart. You should be able to feel the pressure of the water against your hand. This 'feel' is very important for all swimming strokes. When you swim you should be able to feel the pressure of the water on your hand constantly. If you don't, practise the ∞ movement often.

In freestyle the hand should enter the water at arm's length just off the centre line (between your nose and shoulder). Once entered, the arm extends to maximum length and once there, begins the S shape arm pull. The arm pulls down and slightly outward, then in under your chest, and out past your thigh to full extension. After completing this S shape stroke you begin the arm recovery stage.

Arm recovery The arm recovery varies from swimmer to swimmer. The most important factor is to have a relaxed movement of your arm from the stroke to the beginning of the next stroke, keeping your elbow higher than your hand and your hand close to the water.

Breathing There are two types of breathing — alternate breathing every arm cycle (two strokes) and bi-lateral breathing. Alternate means the swimmer breathes at the complete arm cycle, e.g. to the left side, then to the right side and then to the left etc. Bi-lateral means breathing to both sides, taking a breath every third arm stroke.

Breathing preference is an individual choice, however, bi-lateral breathing encourages good body roll. Over a period of time swimmers who only breathe on one side tend to develop an uneven style, leaning on one arm, therefore losing valuable efficiency. A combination of both breathing patterns is best.

When to breathe As your left arm extends into your stroke, turn your head slightly to the right so that ⅔ of your face is out of the water. When you breathe on the right it will be as the right hand passes underneath the shoulder, and then the hand travels out past the thigh. With a relaxed opening of the mouth, take a breath and turn your head back into the water. Slowly breathe out during the next few arm strokes until the next breath. Do not hold your breath.

Practise breathing movements while standing in waist deep water before deciding which breathing pattern is best for you.

Body roll The body moves through the water best when on its side. Imagine your body is on a skewer. Your body should then roll evenly and in a controlled manner at about 45 degrees to each side.

There are many books that explain all swimming strokes in detail. Enrol in a class with qualified coaches if you want to learn all strokes. Although butterfly looks much harder, it is just as easy to learn as breaststroke and backstroke.

DESIGNING A PROGRAM

Where you begin on this program will depend upon your starting level. The table below will indicate where it is appropriate for you to start:

ACTIVITY LEVEL	SUGGESTED STARTING POINT
• Cannot breaststroke 50 m	Seek lessons from a qualified coach until able to swim 50 m breaststroke
• Can swim 50 m breaststroke; cannot freestyle 100 m	**Getting Started**
• Can swim 50 m breaststroke, can swim 100 m freestyle	**Keeping it Going**
• Can swim 1.2 km freestyle continuously	**Getting Better**

GETTING STARTED
FREQUENCY: 3–4 × week

START AT:	BUILD TO:
50 m breaststroke warm up	50 m freestyle warm up
(25 m freestyle + 25 m breaststroke) × 4	(50 m freestyle + 50 m breaststroke) × 2
rest after each 50 m	rest after each 50 m
50 m breaststroke slow	50 m freestyle × 4
	50 m freestyle slow
	50 m freestyle × 4
50 m breaststroke slow	50 m freestyle slow

KEEPING IT GOING
FREQUENCY: 3–5 × week

START AT:
100 m freestyle warm up
50 m freestyle × 6
10 seconds rest after each 50 m
300 m freestyle continuous

BUILD TO:
100 m freestyle warm up
100 m freestyle × 4
30 seconds rest after each 100 m
200 m freestyle × 2 (4 mins each)

Getting Better

This program has a slightly different format from the previous two. The basic program is similar in that it is based on interval swimming with rests in between each repeat. Also included is one session per week of long slow distance swimming, designed to improve the quality of the aerobic base.

BASIC PROGRAM
FREQUENCY: 3–4 × week

START AT:
100 m freestyle warm up
100 m × 6
30 seconds rest after each 100 m
200 m × 2
30 seconds rest after each 200 m
100 freestyle slow

BUILD TO:
100 m freestyle warm up
2 km in less than 38 mins
100 m freestyle slow

LONG SLOW DISTANCE PROGRAM
FREQUENCY: 1 × week

START AT:
1.2 km slow and continuous

BUILD TO:
3.0 km slow and continuous

Taking It Further

The serious swimmer may wish to train for competition in either club or triathlon events. It would then be necessary to include shorter (anaerobic) swim sessions in your weekly program. These would be introduced at the **Getting Better** level.

ANAEROBIC PROGRAM
FREQUENCY: 2 × week

START AT:
200 m freestyle warm up
(25 m fast + 25 m slow) × 10
10 seconds rest after each 50 m
100 m freestyle slow

BUILD TO:
200 m freestyle warm up
100 m fast × 8
3 minutes rest after each 100 m
50 m fast × 8
90 seconds rest after each 50 m
100 m freestyle slow

If you want to dive with goggles, make sure that your arms are stretched in a streamlined position over your ears when you enter the water. Tuck your chin onto your chest so that the water hits the top of the head and not the forehead. Practice makes perfect.

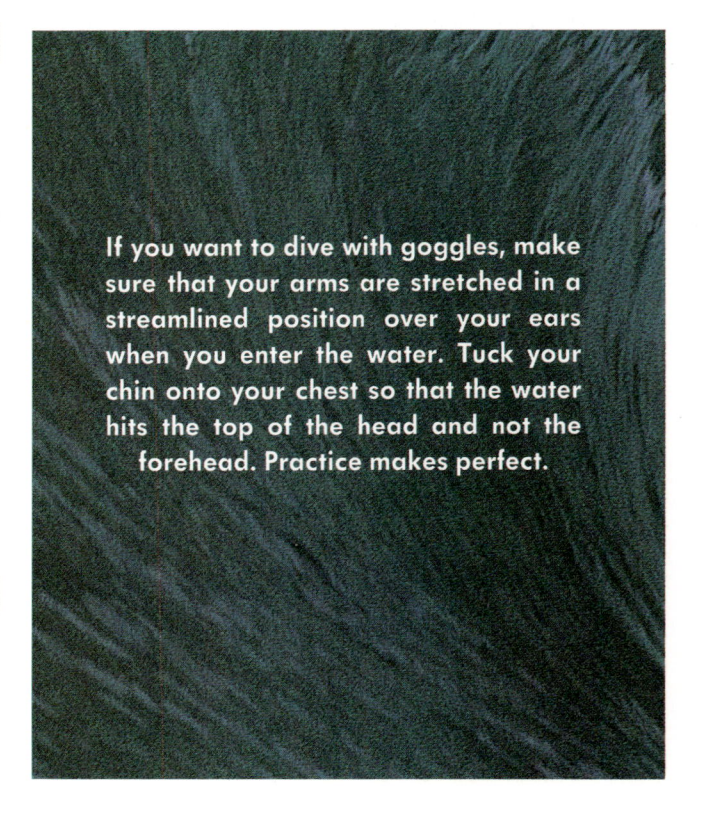

LISA CURRY : PERSONAL PROFILE

One very hot and humid day when it was too hot to go to my weekly jazz ballet class, I went swimming at a nearby pool. The local coach at the pool was Harry Gallagher — a top Australian swim coach. He was coaching his squad when I dived in for a swim. Seeing my flailing arms and legs, he came and asked me to swim a lap for him. He then asked if I was interested in joining his squad. I was ten years old. Harry came to our house to talk to Mum and Dad. He told them I would have to have my teeth straightened because one day I would be Australia's fastest 100m freestyler and would have my photo taken a lot. At that age I didn't think too much about it. Not long after though, the 1972 Olympics were held. Shane Gould won three gold medals, and that was all I needed to start me on my way. Soon afterwards I won my first race and had my first disqualification — in butterfly. I then attended private butterfly classes.

When I was twelve, I went to my first age nationals, and came 4th in the 100m freestyle. Harry then moved to Canada, so I had to find another coach. A friend at school suggested Joe King, so I happily changed training venues. I swam in the 1976 Olympic trials and came 5th in the 100m breaststroke and 2nd in the 200m individual medley. That year, however, they took out the 200 medley, so I did not get chosen for the games.

I represented my country for the first time when I was fourteen. I also began to realise the opportunities that were opening up for me — training, competition, motivation, dedication, overseas travel, meeting new people, learning about other cultures, hard work, self esteem, confidence, handling pressure, winning, losing, accepting defeat, sharing, communicating.

There are many things to achieve through sport other than winning gold medals. If you give 100 per cent in everything you do, if you have tried your best — you are a winner. (You only become a loser when you stop trying).

Because so many Australians live very close to the sea, it is important for every child to learn how to swim and to swim well. Being able to swim 25m only is enough to get you into trouble but not enough to get you out of it.

I have been part of an Australian swimming team for thirteen years — all of those with Joe King, who, by the way, cannot swim himself! The respect and admiration I have for Joe is part of my success story. Through my younger years, my tough adolescent years, my college years and now my married years, he has given me unfailing support in good times and in bad. He is an inspiration to all who come in contact with him.

My swimming years, with all their opportunities, the ups and downs, and the learning experiences, will stay with me for the rest of my life. My decision to give it 'one more go' in the 1990 Commonwealth Games, was a personal challenge. I believed I had more to give — I wanted to prove myself that yes, I did retire too early.

I learnt a great deal about myself from the experience, and now believe that whatever you want to do, if you are committed, enthusiastic and single-minded, you can achieve.

All my swimming years were fun but I must say that the 1990 Commonwealth Games and the training required, were the greatest moments of my sporting life. I will never forget them.

Learning how to do a tumble turn will help keep your swimming consistent, but isn't necessary as a fitness component.

If your legs and hips sink, you need to strengthen your kick by doing kick drills. A pull buoy between your legs will also help keep your hips up.

SWIMMING

DESIGNING YOUR FITNESS PROGRAM

SWIMMING

103

AQUA-AEROBICS

When it is just too hot and sticky to exercise, the answer is a water workout. Aqua-aerobics is dance exercises performed in water. It is virtually injury free because the water makes your body weight very low. It is also excellent for those suffering from repetition strain injury.

To organise your own workout:
- Remember the F.I.T. principles.
- Wear a waterproof sunscreen, sunglasses and a hat.
- Draw up A4 size cards with a different exercise on each and place them around your pool. If you laminate them, they won't get damaged.
- Play your favourite music.
- Keep the water level between your stomach and shoulders.
- Use hand paddles for extra resistance.
- 'Feel' the water — the more resistance you feel, the better
- Warm up with a couple of laps of jogging or swimming.
- Stretch your whole body.
- Exercise for at least 30 minutes.
- Warm down with some easy swimming.
- Wear a water resistant watch to monitor your training heart rate and to time your exercises.

AQUA AEROBICS

FIGURE ∞ Stand in fairly deep water with your hands wide apart, palms facing in (as if you are holding something). Push the water, so you can feel the resistance, until the hands come together. Turn your hand, palms facing out and continue to push out. Push in and push out in the figure ∞. Feel the resistance constantly. This is great for toning arms.

DESIGNING YOUR FITNESS PROGRAM

RUNNING IN WATER This is great for athletes who have an injury, as well as for developing extra aerobic fitness. Keep your shoulders just underneath the water. Keep hands flat (like a paddle) for more resistance both forwards and backwards. Lift legs high for more resistance.

SCISSOR KICK Sit up against the wall of the pool, back flat and arms on the side for support. Bring your legs up to hip height, feet flexed, and push out as far as you can and in together. Feel the resistance.

TREAD WATER This will burn many calories if continued for 30 mins or more. Keep your heart rate at moderate pace. For increased heart rate, occasionally lift your arms out of the water. Move your legs vigorously.

PUSH OUTS With hands shoulder width apart – place on the side of the pool (it's better and harder if you can't reach the bottom with your feet). Lift yourself up until your arms are straight — keep elbows 'soft'. Lower yourself back into the water and try not to touch the bottom.

SWIMMING

105

CYCLING

BENEFITS

Cycling develops cardiovascular fitness and assists in weight control. It can be equal to running as an aerobic conditioner, but it also has other benefits. The cyclist is mobile and a cycling program can contain a wider variety of things to do including training, family outings and the opportunity to travel longer distances. This helps to minimise the possibility of boredom.

Cyclists generally do not suffer from the stress injuries that runners can experience. Cycling is low-impact or non weight-bearing and is therefore suitable for those who are overweight or susceptible to stress injury. Cycling injuries are usually minor and careful programming, good technique, proper equipment and clothing can prevent or minimise them.

MUSCLES WORKED

Cycling works most of the major muscles in your legs and buttocks and has some benefit for your arms and shoulders.

CYCLE IT OFF!

ACTIVITY LEVEL	KILOJOULES (CALORIES) PER 30 MINUTES
9 km/hr	489 (111)
16 km/hr	828 (198)
21 km/hr	1205 (288)

EQUIPMENT

Choice of bicycle Before you buy a bicycle you need to consider:

1. How much riding you intend to include in your program (e.g. once a week or every day).
2. What type of riding you intend to do (e.g., ride to work daily, touring, triathlons).
3. Your budget.

There are several types of bike available and your answers to the above questions will determine which one suits you. A typical lightweight racing bike has dropped handlebars, narrow tyres with no guards and a narrow saddle. A touring bike is heavier and more stable, and is designed for travelling long distances with heavier loads. A recreational bike is between the two — heavier than a racer, lighter than a tourer — and its versatility makes it suitable for most people. Also available is a stationary cycle for home use with adjustable resistance, handlebars and odometers. Your racing or touring bike can also be attached to a roller device to convert it to a stationary cycle for a home workout.

Frame type Although frames come in both 'men's' and 'women's' styles, the men's style is stronger and is the better choice. They are made from either tubular aluminium or chrome molybdenum, which is thicker at the ends than in the middle.

Frame size To determine the correct size for you, straddle the top bar with your feet flat on the floor. The frame should be about 2 cm below the crotch. When you sit on the saddle your knee should be slightly bent with your heel on the pedal at its lowest point.

Wheels As with the frame, lighter wheels make for easier riding. Alloy wheels are both light and strong. Look for a quick-release front wheel, it has many advantages, such as easy transportation.

Saddle These come in a range of shapes, sizes and materials. Choose one designed for women. A plastic saddle is practical and resistant to weather. If you intend riding more than 40 km per day, choose a leather one as it stays cooler and forms into the shape of your seat after a few rides.

Handlebars The dropped handlebars are probably the best style as they allow greater variety in body positions, an important consideration on a long ride. This allows you to use some muscle groups while relaxing others.

Gears These enable you to keep your peddling speed fairly constant over a variety of terrains. The more gears you have, the greater the flexibility. Choose a bike with ten gears. This has five gear sprockets in a cluster on the back wheel and two larger ones at the pedals. The gear levers and derailleurs enable you to change from one gear to another.

Extras Provision can be made for a pump, a repair kit, and a water bottle. This is essential equipment, particularly on a long ride. Also carry some change with you, for a possible 'rescue' phone call.

Cycling shorts These are almost a necessity, especially on long rides. They are usually made of lycra or polyester, are longer to protect the legs from friction with the saddle, and have a chamois or towelling padded liner to act as a cushion.

Cycling shoes A serious competitive cyclist would purchase stiff cycling shoes. They are not necessary for the recreational or touring cyclist as they are difficult to walk in. A pair of rubber-soled shoes with a firm rather than a flexible sole would be suitable.

Helmet This is a necessary item, particularly if you intend to ride in traffic. Choose one that is well-ventilated, lightweight, has good shock-absorbing qualities and conforms to the Safety Standards Council recommendations.

Gloves Ones which have padded palms, fingertip openings, and open weave tops for ventilation are comfortable but not really necessary for shorter distance cycling.

Braking The front brake is the one most often used for slowing down as it has the most stopping power. When braking, shift your body weight slightly backwards in the saddle to prevent being thrown over the handlebars.

Terrain and Cadence For the first few weeks you should cycle on flat terrain at a smooth cadence (pedal speed) of about 55–60 rpm (revolutions per minute: one complete circle of the leg is one revolution). As your fitness improves increase the cadence to 70–80 rpm while maintaining a smooth technique. (Remember to take your pulse regularly to ensure you are within your training zone). At this point, include some hills in your workout to practise changing gears.

Extra Stretches

Do stretches particularly for the neck, shoulders, lower back, hamstring, quads, calf and hips.

Technique

Posture Don't slouch. Bend from the waist with your back fairly straight and arms and shoulders relaxed. This forward leaning position helps distribute your weight more evenly over the bike and reduces wind resistance. A position that is too upright is very tiring. Bending the elbows in a relaxed manner helps absorb the shock of road bumps and enables you to develop more power for pedalling, particularly uphill, through better leverage. Grip handlebars at shoulder width.

Gear changes Change down into a lower gear while you are pedalling and before you start to climb a hill rather than when you are on it. Choose a gear suitable to the steepness of a hill, which will enable you to maintain your cadence. Lean forward over the handlebars, but look ahead not downwards. (For steep hills you may need to stand up on the pedals to put extra weight into each pedal stroke). When riding downhill, change to a higher gear and maintain your cadence rather than coasting down. This gives you and your bike more stability.

Designing A Program

	GETTING STARTED	GETTING BETTER	KEEPING IT GOING
START AT:			
F	3 × week	3 × week	4 × week
I	flat terrain (cycle 5 mins, coast 1 min) × 3	flat terrain, some gentle hills (cycle 10 mins, coast 1 min) × 3	flat terrain cycle 30 mins hilly terrain cycle 30 mins
T	approx 20 mins	approx 30 mins	60 mins
BUILD TO:			
F	4 × week	4 × week	4–5 × week
I	flat terrain (cycle 8 mins, coast 1 min) × 3	flat terrain, some gentle hills (cycle 20 mins, coast 1 min) × 3	variable terrain
T	approx 30 mins	approx 60 mins	greater than 60 mins

Taking It Further

Once your reach the **Keeping it Going** stage you should have attained a level of fitness at which you could consider some touring. Start with half-day trips and build to a day trip of anything up to 140 kilometres.

Remember, your legs need to become 'cycle-fit' and your seat has to become accustomed to being in the saddle for longer and longer periods of time. To attempt a long tour before your body is ready will make you feel stiff and sore for several days.

AEROBIC DANCE

Aerobic dance (or aerobics, as it is often called) combines rhythmic exercise, dance steps, running and jumping to form a varied, interesting and lively workout that is performed to music.

Benefits

Aerobic dance improves fitness and health especially when performed vigorously. Many people join aerobic dance classes to lose weight, although weight loss as a direct effect of participation may only be fairly small. Include other low intensity activities such as walking in your program. Two or three aerobics sessions per week will enhance weight loss by keeping your metabolic rate high.

Aerobic dance exercises the whole body. The muscles and joints are moved through a wide range of positions. This develops flexibility, muscular endurance and co-ordination to a greater extent than activities like running, cycling or swimming.

The added bonus of aerobic dance is its liveliness and group orientation. The variety of movements and music are fun and will inspire you to be active.

Muscles Worked

Because of the variety, every muscle is given a workout.

Dance It Off!

Activity Level	Kilojoules (Calories) per 30 minutes
light	452 (108)
moderate	628 (150)
vigorous	1130 (270)

Equipment

Footwear The choice of footwear is an important decision. Running shoes are not suitable as they are designed with their shock-absorbency in the heel.

In contrast an aerobics shoe requires shock absorbency in the forefoot to cushion the many landings on the ball of the foot, and for support during sideways movements. Never perform aerobic dance in bare feet.

Surface If a gym has only concrete floors or carpet-covered concrete, the chances of stress injuries are increased. Instead, look for a gym that conducts its classes on a wooden floor, or at least on a dense rubber surface.

Instructor It is wise to assess the quality of instruction at your gym. Poor instruction is one of the principal causes of any injury sustained during aerobic dance. A class should be fun. Non-smiling faces will soon disappear to a more enjoyable environment.

Extra Stretches

A five-minute stretch session should be part of all good aerobic classes. Concentrate on all body parts. Warm down with suitable stretching. Question a class that has no concluding static stretching.

Technique

Never attempt too much too soon. Because aerobics involves such a wide range of movements, your muscles and joints need the time to get used to them gradually.

A trend has developed towards low-impact aerobics in the wake of injury related to aerobics. This involves a larger proportion of exercises for the upper body, and retains one foot on the floor at all times. It was previously thought that low-impact aerobics produced a smaller cardiovascular effect. However, by employing multi-directional, full body movements (i.e. moving around the room as much as possible with stepping and sliding actions and frequent changes of direction) it is possible to achieve your training heart rate zone. You must also emphasise the use of large muscle groups such as those in the legs, hips and back.

Designing A Program

There are many different types of classes available. Check with your gym to see what they can offer. Most gyms will have programs that fit into the **Getting Started, Getting Better** and **Keeping it Going** guidelines. You will have a choice between high and low impact aerobics, and some more specialised gyms may offer stretch classes and special classes for pregnant women, and for the recovery period after pregnancy.

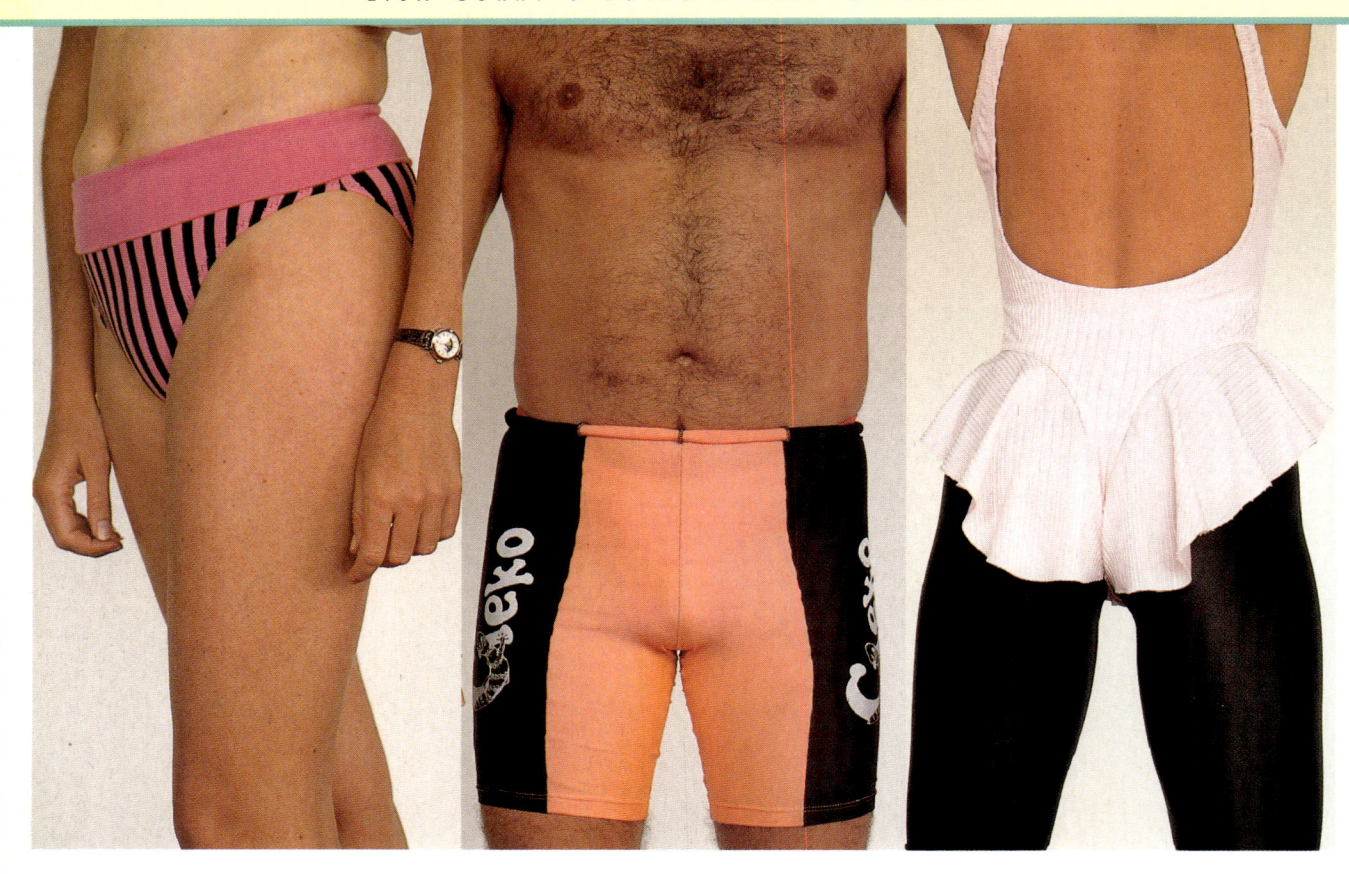

BETWEEN THE BELLY BUTTON AND THE KNEES

Women and men tend to store fat in different parts of their bodies. Women naturally store it around the hips, bottom and thighs, whereas men store fat around their middle and upper back. You can't spot reduce by dieting, but you can reshape these areas with an overall body toning program. The bottom and thighs are a group of very large muscles. To work them is quite difficult, consequently women often quit before they give their body a chance. At aerobic classes many women will do countless numbers of side leg raisers. Most thigh workouts use the outer thigh muscle. What you really need to do is strengthen the inner thigh. These adductor muscles aren't used much, so target this exercise during your gym class. To isolate the inner thigh when doing a lunge, concentrate on pulling your legs together rather than pushing off with your lunging leg. To feel your inner thighs working, lie on the floor with your knees bent and place a plastic ball between your knees. Squeeze the ball to feel the inner thigh muscles working out. Use an adduction/abduction machine if you have access to one. Dead lifts are also good for your legs and thighs.

Sit-ups give you abdominal strength, which in turn provides excellent postural support. This can help prevent and treat lower back trouble. Learn how to perform a series of sit-ups that develops all groups of abdominal muscles.

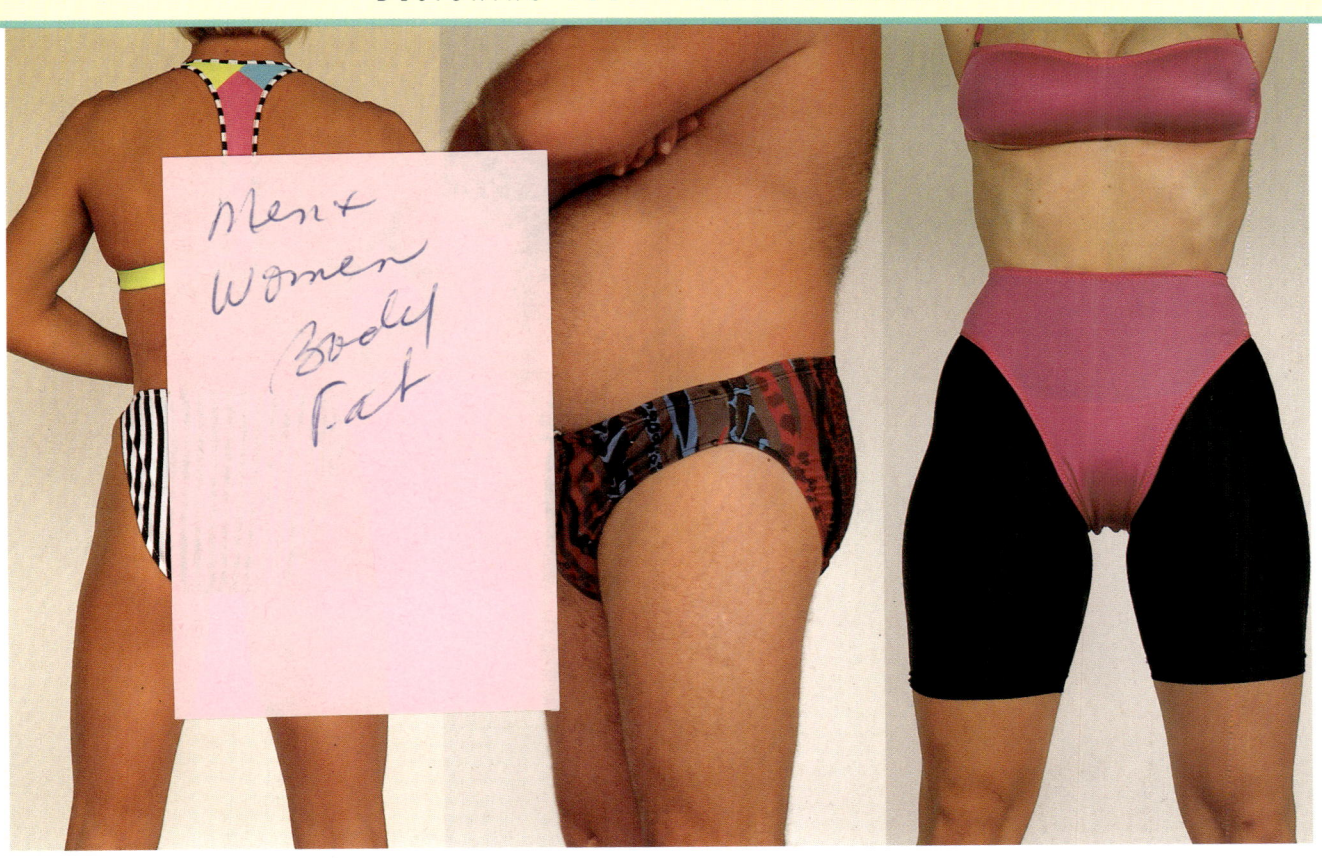

DESIGNING YOUR FITNESS PROGRAM

Men + Women Body Fat

Lie flat on the ground, lower back into the floor, bring your feet flat on the ground as close to your bottom as possible. Fold your arms across your chest, look straight ahead and lift up to about 45 degrees. To work your obliques, bend left knee, put right foot on left knee and bend sideways so that your left elbow aims for your right ankle. To work your lower abdominals, lie flat, press lower back into the ground, lift both legs until vertical and cross them at the feet. Lift your bottom off the ground.

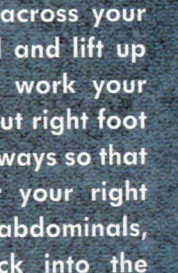

You should become proficient at sit-ups with practice. Performed correctly, sit-ups will help strengthen the back and tone the tummy.

AEROBIC DANCE

113

Taking It Further

As you progress to the **Getting Better** and **Keeping it Going** stages, add wrist weights for extra kilojoule usage. Classes can also use equipment such as dumbbells, rubber bands, balls and hoops. Circuit and combination classes are widely available.

SIT UP
- back flat
- feet close to bottom
- head in line with spine
- eyes forward
- vary arm position for degree of difficulty

SQUAT
- keep heels flat on the ground
- keep knees in line with feet
- bottom only goes as low as parallel to the ground; any further increases the risk of knee injury
- head up, back flat — stay controlled

STAR JUMP
- knees in line with feet
- keep knees 'soft', e.g. slightly bent
- when arms move above shoulder height, keep palms of hands facing forwards (less strain on deltoids)

SIDE TWIST
- when twisting to one side, lift the opposite heel and pivot on the toes — prevents strain being placed on the knee

DESIGNING YOUR FITNESS PROGRAM

WEIGHT TRAINING

There are many varieties of weight training programs, with different combinations of sets and weights to be lifted. The following program is just one example and should be used only as a guide. It is best to be advised by an instructor at your local gym. They will help tailor a weight training program to your individual needs.

BENEFITS

Weight training, sometimes called body toning or sculpting, is an activity within the reach of everyone irrespective of age or ability. You can enjoy health and fitness benefits as well as an improvement in strength in a relatively short time.

Weight training contributes to weight control by maintaining and developing muscle tissue. Muscle tissue has a higher metabolic rate (burns more kilojoules) than fat tissue.

Weight training is used for a variety of purposes. The program you follow will vary according to the specific outcome required. Most people are familiar with the competitive sport of weightlifting where the athlete attempts to lift as heavy a weight as possible using clearly defined movements. Body builders use weight training methods to develop large and well-defined muscles. Sports medicine practitioners recommend forms of weight training to rehabilitate injured muscles and joints. Athletes, both competitive and recreational, use weight training to increase strength for improved performance in a variety of sports. These strength gains will enable you to perform all tasks much more easily.

Weight training itself is not an aerobic exercise and should be combined with aerobic activities, such as those already mentioned, as part of total fitness plan.

115

MUSCLES WORKED

You can work any muscles you choose. If you look in a weight training gym you may notice that women tend to work on their thighs and buttocks while men work on their arms, chest and shoulders. For an overall toning effect women should work on their upper body as well. Full body strength can be a great advantage. Combined with good posture it provides a positive effect on self image.

LIFT IT OFF!

ACTIVITY LEVEL	KILOJOULES (CALORIES) PER 30 MINUTES
moderate	1796(429)

EQUIPMENT

Most people who take up weight training do so in gyms equipped for the purpose and with instructors who are willing to assist the newcomer get under way. The alternative is to have your own equipment at home. There are advantages and disadvantages in both. It is advisable to start out at a gym so that you learn correct technique. This will also help you to decide which equipment is most suited to you.

Weights There are basically two types of equipment — free weights and machines. Most gyms will have both types. It is possible to structure a suitable program using either form, but a combination of the two is best. The standard free weight equipment consists of a bar with weights (or plates) added to each end and secured by collars. Dumbbells are also free weights. They are intended for use in pairs, have fixed plates and come in a range of weights.

Machines such as Universal, Nautilus, Hydragym or Titan are excellent weight training equipment, though they are generally too expensive for home use. They have either a stack of weights or hydraulic pressure that can be increased or decreased according to the needs of the exercise. They allow the exercise movement to be performed in a controlled way.

Clothing It is not necessary to wear special clothing for weight training. All you need are comfortable clothes that allow a full range of movement and sports shoes with a sole that prevents slipping. Gloves may be used for free weights.

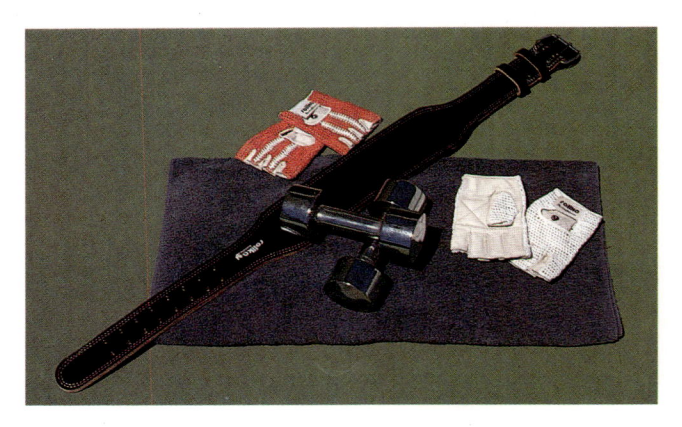

Weight Belt Wearing a weight belt will protect the lower back when performing squats and cleans with weights.

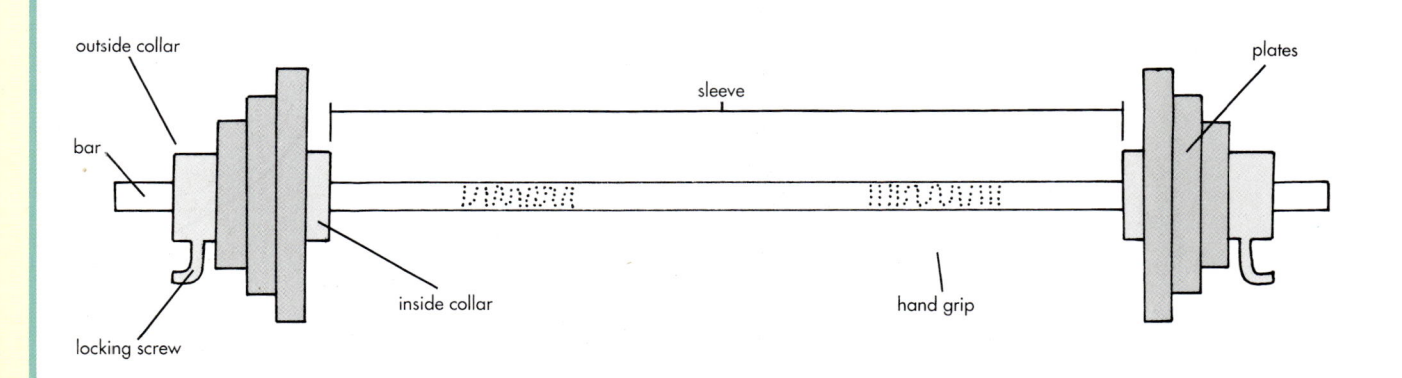

Extra Stretches

It is wise to stretch the muscle groups just worked within three seconds of completing a set of repetitions. This allows maximum lengthening of that muscle and will help prevent soreness. Hold the stretch for 10–15 seconds. Stretch both sides.

Technique

Use the correct technique as explained for each exercise.

Terminology

Weight training has a number of terms which need to be defined in order to make sense of the program details.

Load This is the weight (or resistance) to be lifted and is usually measured in kilograms.

Repetition Maximum (RM) This refers to a load that can be lifted a certain number of times, e.g. 6 RM is a load that can be lifted a maximum of six times, 12 RM can be lifted a maximum of 12 times etc.

Repetitions (reps) This refers to the number of times the load is lifted. A program with a load of 6 RM will have sets consisting of 6 repetitions, 12 RM sets will have 12 repetitions.

Set This is a grouping of a number of repetitions, e.g. a set may consist of 6 reps or 10 reps etc.

Circuits Weight training is usually performed in circuit fashion; that is, there is a list of say ten exercises done one after the other, where the lifter performs one set of each. At the end of the first circuit there is a short rest of between 2–4 minutes, followed by a second set of each exercise, then a third set to finish.

Training Objectives

Your reasons for including weight training in your weekly schedule will largely determine the type of program you follow and the exercises to be included. There is an endless variety to choose from and it is therefore difficult to prescribe a program to suit everyone. If you wish to use weight

WEIGHT TRAINING

training for body building or weightlifting, then it will be necessary for you to consult a more specialist text (see page 169).

This program concentrates on strength, power and endurance. The methods used to meet each of these objectives have some similarities, but the difference is the load lifted and the speed with which it is lifted. Because power and endurance have a strength component it is necessary to develop strength first and then convert the strength gains to power and/or endurance by altering the load lifted. Before strength gains are developed, it is usual for a beginner to start on a general program that tones up the whole body and prepares the muscles for the heavier lifting needed to build strength.

The following RMs are suitable for development of each training objective:

General Program	12 RM
Strength Development	1–6 RM
Power Development	10–12 RM
Endurance	15–25 RM

Some women are concerned that with weight training they may develop unwanted muscle tissue and a masculine appearance. However, the growth of muscles is determined by the male hormone testosterone, and the low levels of this found in women tend to limit the amount of muscle development. However, considerable strength gains can be achieved and the reduction in body fat results in a better toned body, which looks and feels great.

Although you can't spot reduce — the weight you lose will come off all parts of your body — you can spot train. This reshapes the body part through weight training.

SAFETY PRECAUTIONS

- Warm up
- Use the correct technique as explained for each exercise
- If you have any difficulties with an exercise, seek the assistance of your gym instructor who is qualified to advise you on correct technique
- Ensure collars are tight when using free weights
- Learn correct breathing technique
- Avoid dangerous exercises
- Progress slowly

DESIGNING A PROGRAM

GENERAL POINTS

Three sets provide optimum development irrespective of your training objectives. Three times per week on alternate days is the best frequency for weight training. Those who want to work out more should exercise the upper body on one day and lower body the next. This allows each muscle group to have the necessary time for recovery.

Vary exercises to maintain interest. You can substitute another exercise that works the same muscle group for those in the program. An instructor can assist here.

Set yourself long- and short-term goals and keep a record of your workouts.

Working with a partner helps to keep you both motivated. It is also an added safety precaution. Your partner can assist by lifting and replacing weights for you in exercises such as the bench press.

Working with music in the background can make your workout more enjoyable.

GETTING STARTED

This is designed to introduce you to weight training. It is a general body conditioner and prepares you for the levels to follow.

HALF SQUAT
QUADRICEPS, GLUTEUS, HAMSTRINGS

1ST POSITION
- feet shoulder width apart
- knees slightly bent
- back flat
- head up, eyes forward (not down)

2ND POSITION
- keep heels on the ground
- slowly and with control, bend at the knees and lower your body to the floor in a vertical position. Keep looking straight ahead
- lower about 6–8 inches
- return to 1st position

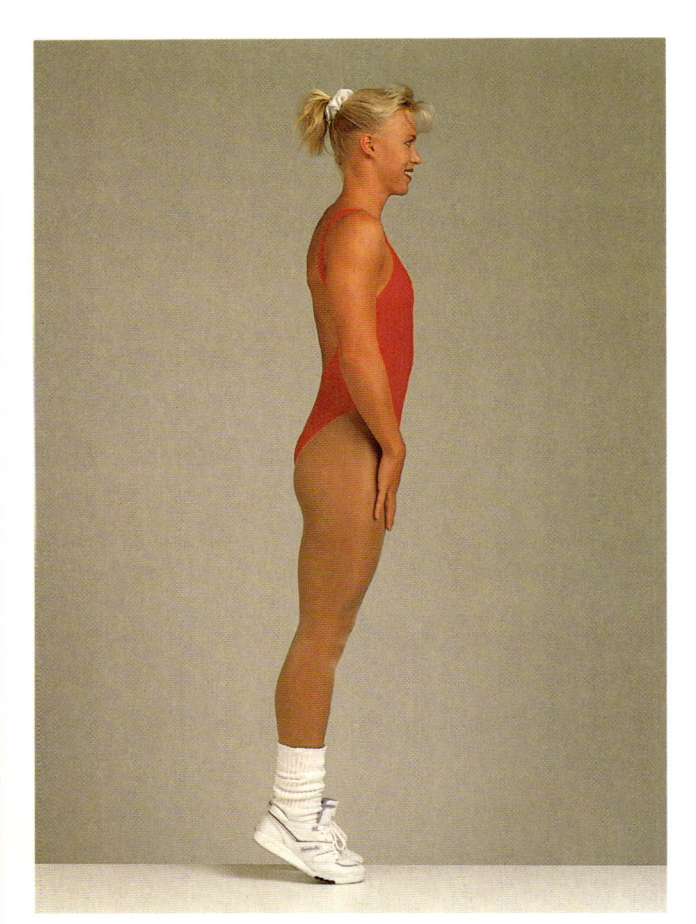

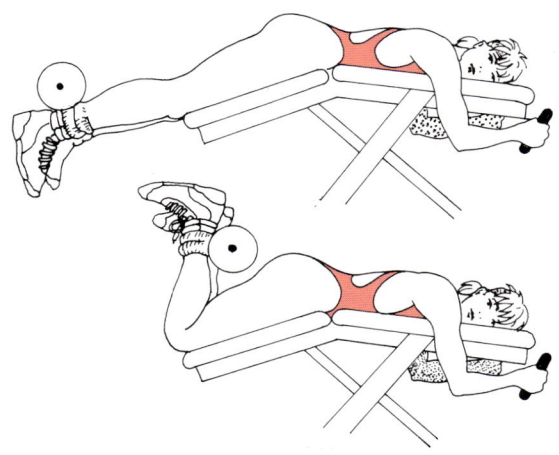

LISA CURRY'S TOTAL HEALTH & FITNESS

LEG CURL / LEG EXTENSION
(QUADRICEPS, HAMSTRINGS)

NB These can be done on a variety of machines together or separately

1ST POSITION
- sit comfortably
- hang onto machine
- feet flexed (toes towards body); pull the weight up in a slow and controlled way

2ND POSITION
- feet still flexed
- push the weight down in a slow and controlled way

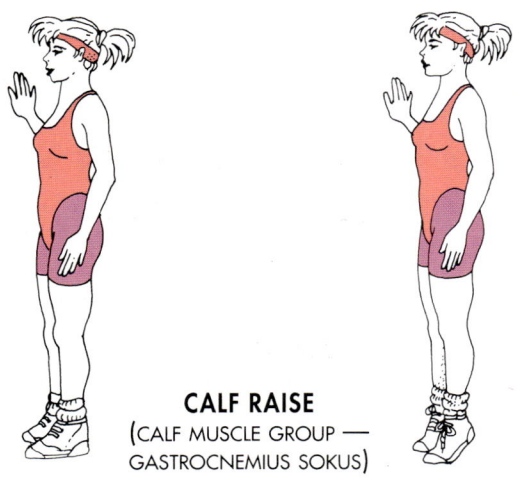

CALF RAISE
(CALF MUSCLE GROUP — GASTROCNEMIUS SOKUS)

1ST POSITION
- stand with good posture, eyes forward; support yourself if necessary
- feet flat on the floor, about 6 inches apart

2ND POSITION
- rise upwards onto your toes; legs straight
- return to 1st position — use weights if you want to work harder

NB Do more repetitions on calves because they are a smaller muscle group

WEIGHT TRAINING

120

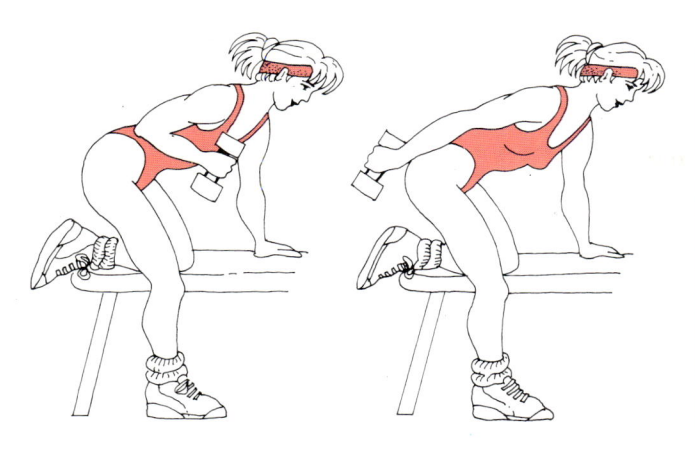

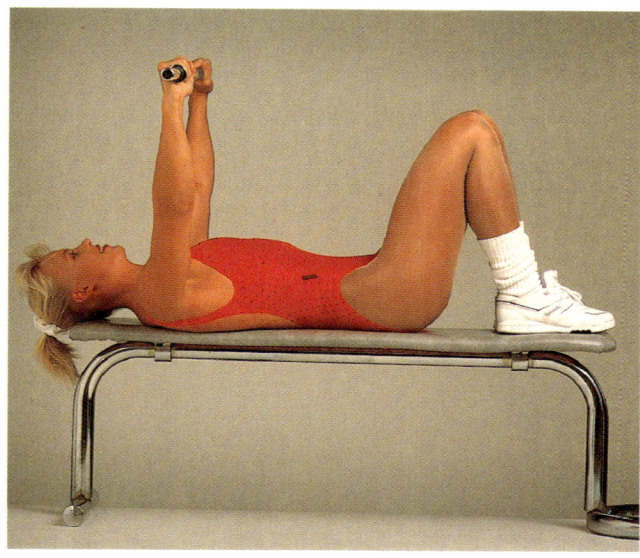

DESIGNING YOUR FITNESS PROGRAM

TRICEP PRESS
(TRICEP)

1ST POSITION
- support on bench
- one knee on bench, other leg slightly bent on floor
- back flat
- eyes forward
- elbow tucked into side

2ND POSITION
- extend arm fully in a controlled manner; keep elbow in
- return to 1st position
- work both arms

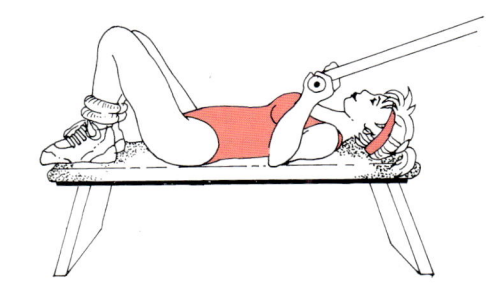

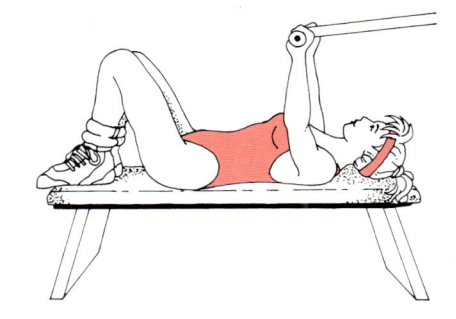

BENCH PRESS
(PECTORALS MAJOR)

1ST POSITION
- lie flat on bench
- back flat (especially lower back)
- feet flat onto bench, close to buttocks
- eyes up
- elbows shoulder height
- hand grip elbow width
- bar horizontal just above chest

2ND POSITION
- push straight up
- don't lock up — keep elbows 'soft' (just slightly bent)
- return to 1st position

WEIGHT TRAINING

121

LISA CURRY'S TOTAL HEALTH & FITNESS

WEIGHT TRAINING

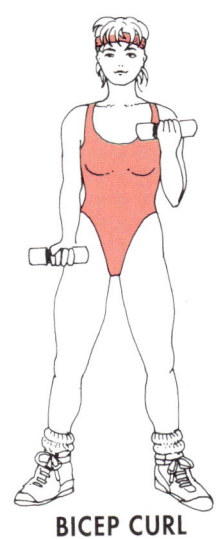

BICEP CURL
(OVERALL BICEPS)

1st Position
- stand with good posture
- feet shoulder width apart
- knees slightly bent
- elbows close to body
- lift one arm/hand to shoulder

2nd Position
- alternate lifting one arm after the other
- lower to touch leg

LAT PULLDOWN
(LATISSIMUS DORSI)

1st Position
- sit comfortably
- wide grip on bar
- back flat

2nd position
- pull bar down — to the front or to the back of the neck

122

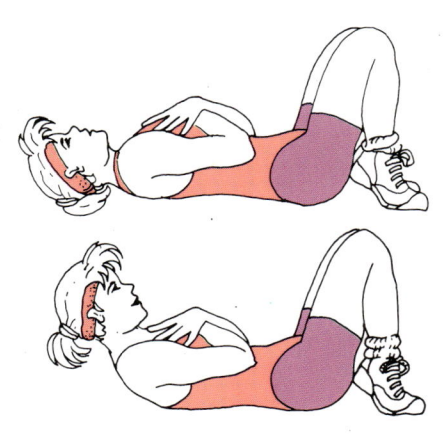

DESIGNING YOUR FITNESS PROGRAM

Allow a short rest between each exercise. This time will enable you to adjust the weights and get used to the order of exercises performed at this level.

GETTING BETTER

This is designed to build on the condition developed in **Getting Started.** It will serve as a basis for the next level.

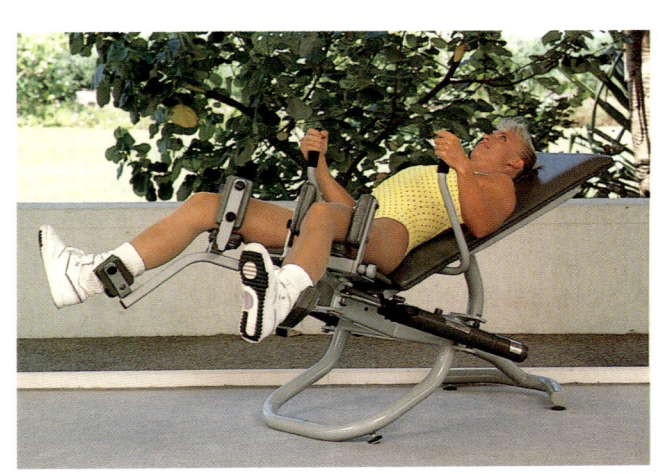

ABDOMINALS 1
(UPPER ABDOMINALS)

1ST POSITION
- lie flat on floor or bench
- flat back
- feet close to buttocks and together (lift heels — optional)
- arms crossed on chest
- head in line with body
- eyes to the ceiling

2ND POSITION
- lift shoulders off ground about 6 inches; keep controlled and remain
- return to 1st position

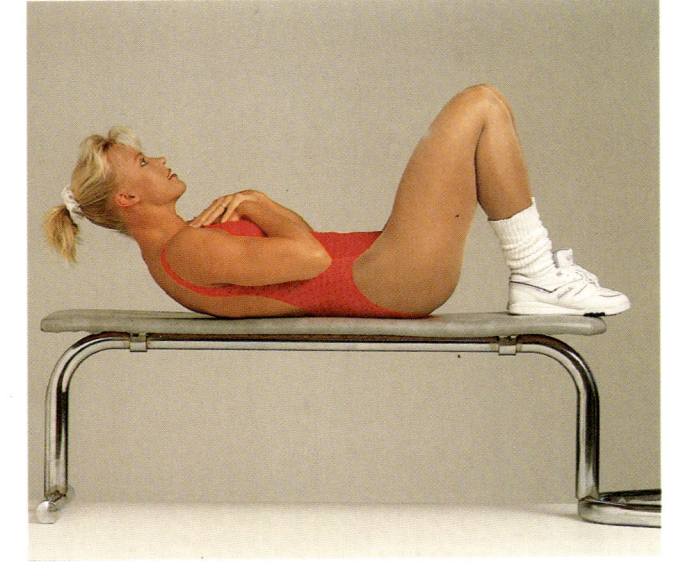

For the first two sessions use barbells with a very light resistance to learn correct technique. Perform 3 sets of 10 repetitions for each exercise in the circuit. During the third session, establish your 12 RM (that is, the weight you can just lift 12 times — this is your training load) and start from there.

LEG ADDUCTION/ABDUCTION
(INNER AND OUTER THIGH)
(ABDUCTOR: LONGUS, MAGNUS, BREVIS)

1ST POSITION
- lie flat and relaxed
- feet flexed
- head, shoulders on bench

2ND POSITION
- push legs wide
- keep feet flexed
- pull legs together to 1st position

WEIGHT TRAINING

123

LISA CURRY'S TOTAL HEALTH & FITNESS

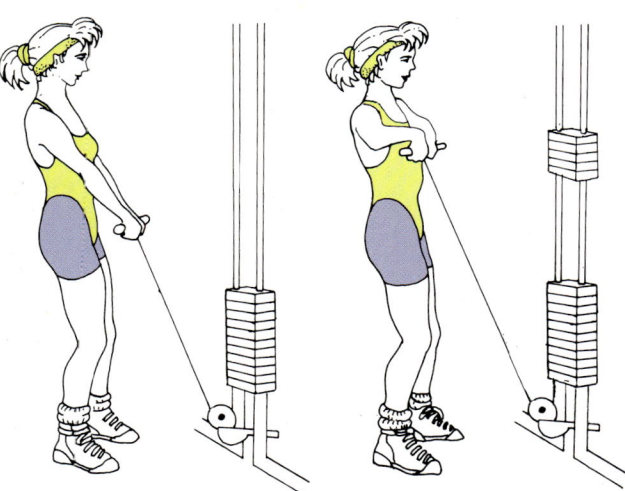

WEIGHT TRAINING

UPRIGHT SHOULDER ROW
(FRONT DELTOIDS AND TRAPEZIUS — WITH NARROW GRIP — SIDE DELTOIDS AND TRAPEZIUS WITH WIDE GRIP)

1ST POSITION
- stand with good posture
- feet shoulder width apart
- knees slightly bent
- hold onto bar

2ND POSITION
- lift bar until elbows horizontal with shoulders
- slowly return to 1st position

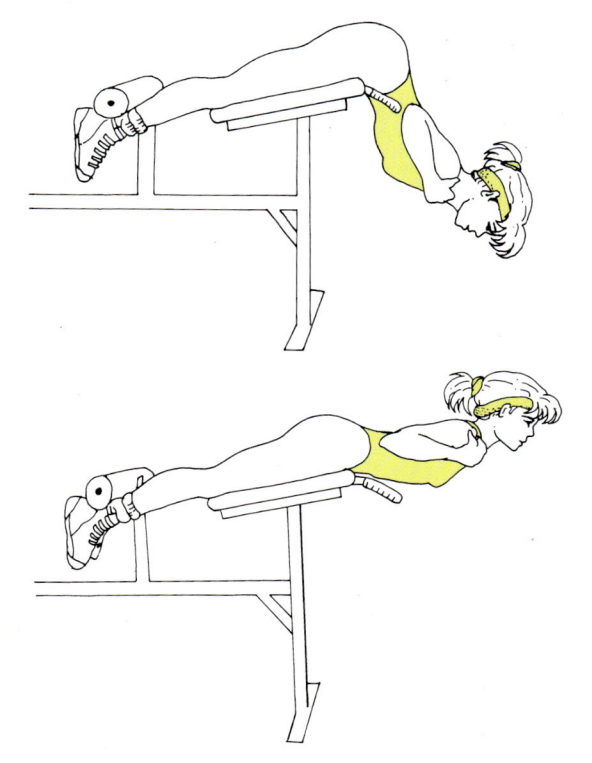

BACK EXTENSION
(HAMSTRINGS, GLUTEUS, LOWER BACK, ERECTOR SPINAE MUSCLE GROUP)

1ST POSITION
- position yourself in back extension machine
- hands touching your shoulders or ears — do not clasp behind head. Advanced people can hold a weight on their chest
- relax with your head near the floor
- feet flexed

2ND POSITION
- rise up until you are parallel to the floor; back flat and straight
- head in line with back
- stay controlled
- return to 1st position

124

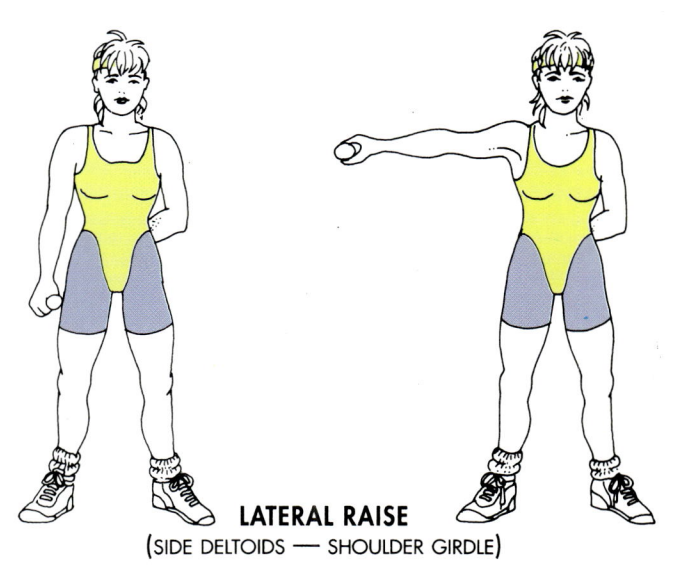

DESIGNING YOUR FITNESS PROGRAM

LATERAL RAISE
(SIDE DELTOIDS — SHOULDER GIRDLE)

1ST POSITION
- good posture
- feet shoulder width apart
- knees slightly bent
- eyes forward and arms close to body; other arm behind back

2ND POSITION
- lift arm close to body to shoulder height
- keep hand facing ground
- return to 1st position
- (work both arms)

SHOULDER SHRUG
(NECK AND SHOULDER) (TRAPEZIUS DELTOIDS)

1ST POSITION
- good posture
- feet shoulder width apart
- knees slightly bent
- eyes forward
- arms close to body
- shoulders level

2ND POSITION
- lift shoulders
- return to 1st position

WEIGHT TRAINING

125

LISA CURRY'S TOTAL HEALTH & FITNESS

ABDOMINALS II
(UPPER ABDOMINALS)

1ST POSITION
- lie flat on floor or bench, back flat
- lower back flat
- head on floor
- arms by side
- feet together and flat close to buttocks
- eyes to ceiling

2ND POSITION
- lift shoulders as far as possible off floor
- arms will move in a straight line towards toes
- keep head still — eyes to ceiling
- return to 1st position

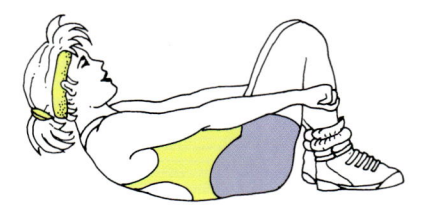

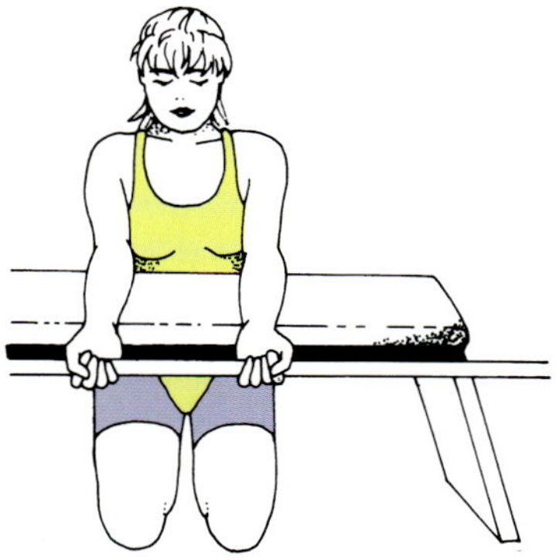

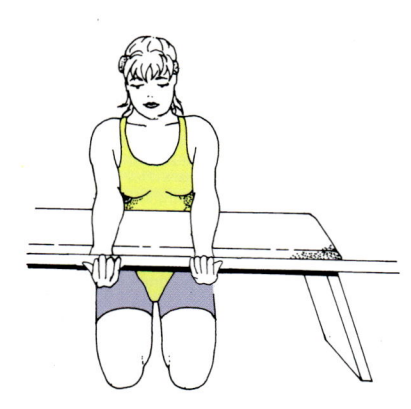

WRIST CURLS
(FOREARMS)

1ST POSITION
- kneel comfortably at bench
- arms at right angle resting on bench and wrists straight in line
- hands free from bench and relax to low position

2ND POSITION
- move only your wrists
- curl weight/bar upwards
- lower to 1st position

NB As with the calf exercises, do more repetitions because they are a small muscle group

WEIGHT TRAINING

126

DESIGNING YOUR FITNESS PROGRAM

Perform three sets of each exercise in a circuit. The load is established this time as 6 RM.

KEEPING IT GOING

This level is designed to allow you to specialise your weight training for a specific purpose. The exercises you choose for this level will depend on your own particular goals. Add the following to your program:

CLEAN
(OVERALL MUSCLE GROUPS, ESPECIALLY UPPER LEG AND BUTTOCKS)

1ST POSITION
- feet shoulder width apart and flat on floor
- back flat
- full squat — buttocks parallel to ground
- hold bar at shoulder width
- head straight
- eyes looking down but forward

2ND POSITION
- lift up and at same time when bar lifts to chest, flick the bar until it rests on your hand
- keep knees slightly bent
- eyes ahead
- return to 1st position

WEIGHT TRAINING

127

LISA CURRY'S TOTAL HEALTH & FITNESS

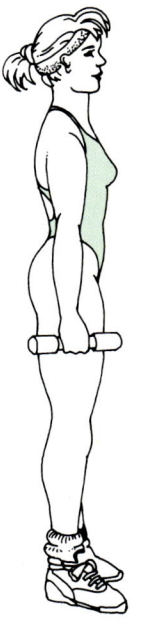

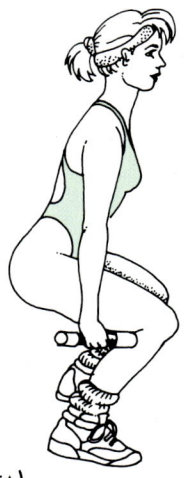

WEIGHT TRAINING

SQUAT II
(ENTIRE THIGH AREA)
(GLUTEUS/QUADS/HAMSTRINGS)

1st Position
- good posture
- feet shoulder width apart
- knees slightly bent
- arms close to body
- looking ahead

2nd Position
- keep feet flat
- slowly lower until buttocks parallel to floor
- back straight, looking ahead
- return to 1st position

LEG RAISE
(LOWER ABDOMINALS)

1st Position
- either on machine or elbows at right angles
- feet flexed
- hang from bar arms, feet flexed

2nd Position
- lift legs until parallel to floor
- lower gently
- do not swing back
- lift legs until knees to chest, lower gently, remain controlled

128

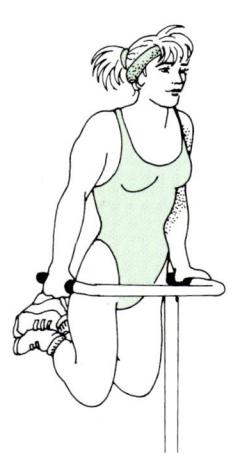

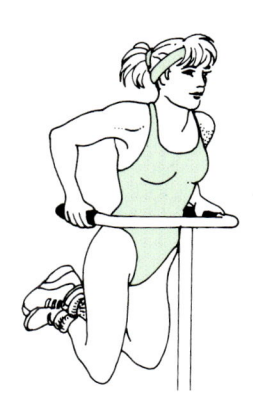

DESIGNING YOUR FITNESS PROGRAM

DIPS
(LOWER, OUTER PECTORALS, DELTOIDS, TRICEPS)

1ST POSITION
- push yourself up into start position
- wrists straight
- feet crossed (optional)

2ND POSITION
- lower until chest to bar or as far down as possible (beginners on dips, only go a part of the way until stronger)
- return to 1st position
- keep elbows 'soft'. Do not lock up

NB This is a good power and strength exercise for many sports. Lifting your own body weight develops your strength

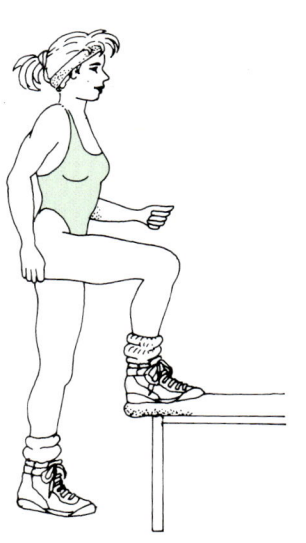

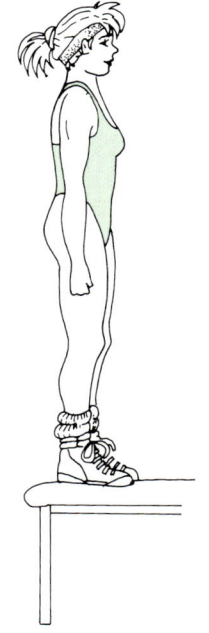

BENCH STEP UP
(QUADRICEPS, HAMSTRINGS, CALVES, GLUTEUS)

1ST POSITION
- good posture
- stand in front on stable bench or box (step on to something higher to work harder)
- step one foot on to bench, followed by other foot
- use opposite arms to help
- back straight — eyes forward (not down)

2ND POSITION
- step back down to floor, one foot at a time
- swap leading foot

WEIGHT TRAINING

LISA CURRY'S TOTAL HEALTH & FITNESS

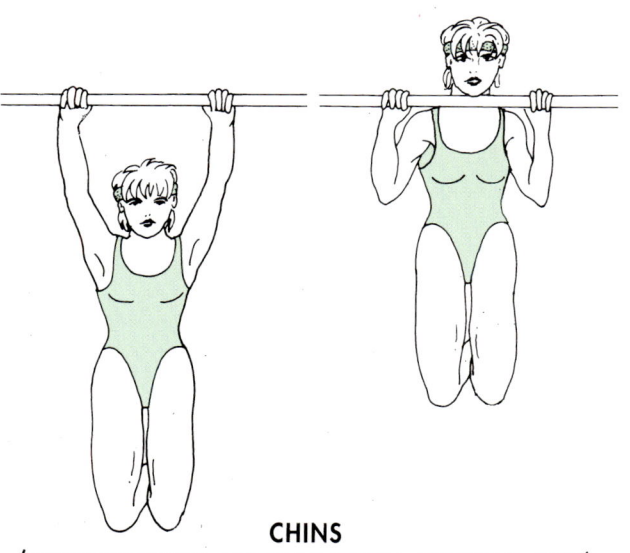

WEIGHT TRAINING

CHINS
(HANDS BACKWARD, LATISSIMUS DORSAL, FOREARMS, BICEP)

1st Position
- hands shoulder width apart
- hands facing either way (depending on what area you want to work)

2nd Position
- feet crossed

- pull your body up until your chin is above the bar
- you can pull your body up with the bar behind your neck also (only hands forward)
- keep knees together
- return to 1st position

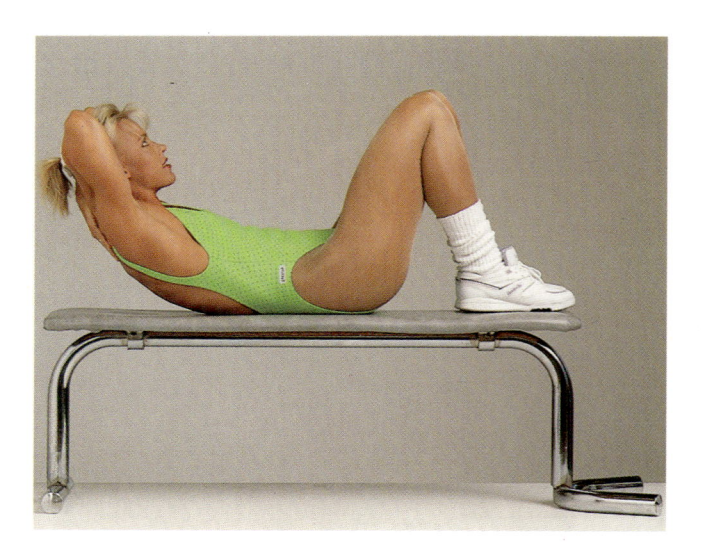

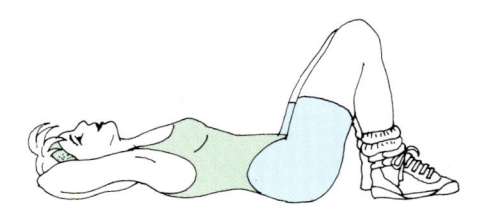

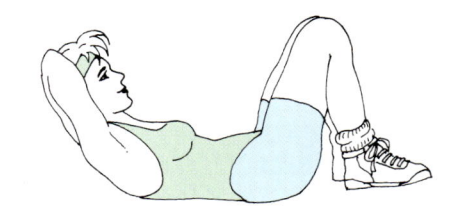

ABDOMINALS III
(UPPER ABDOMINAL WALL)

1st Position
- lie flat on floor or bench
- back flat, lower back flat
- feet together and close to buttocks
- hands crossed on back
- head straight

2nd Position
- lift shoulders as far as possible (won't be very far!)
- eyes to ceiling
- head straight
- lower to 1st position

130

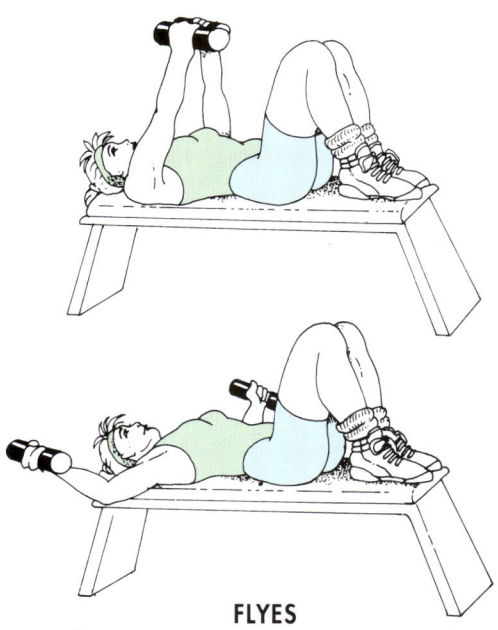

FLYES
(OUTER PECTORALS, ANTERIOR DELTOIDS)

1st Position
- lie flat on bench, back flat
- feet together and close to buttocks
- arms extended out — parallel to ground (do not go down further than shoulder height)

2nd Position
- raise arms up until nearly touching
- lower slowly to 1st position

To develop strength follow the format you used for 6 RM. It is important to lift and lower in a controlled movement. Before power development can proceed, strength must first be improved. In development for a particular sport, this is best done in the off-season.

Power is a necessary characteristic for many competitive sports. Power development should also occur in the pre-season program. During power training, emphasise speed of movement and follow the 12 RM format.

If muscular endurance is required, follow a 20 RM format, emphasising high repetitions and speed of movement.

MUSCLE BUILDING METHODS COMPARED

LIGHT FREE WEIGHTS
These weigh under 2 kilos and either slip, buckle or wrap around wrists, or are small dumbbells held in the hand. Some toning may be visible in upper body. Beginners may notice some strengthening. These weights can be used with aerobic dance to increase kilojoule burning.

RUBBER BANDS
These create resistance with tension not weight. They will add some strength and toning. They are inexpensive and portable enough to travel with.

TWO-KILOGRAM-PLUS FREE WEIGHTS
These include dumbbells and bars with either weights or plates. Strength and muscle building possibilities are endless. They can sculpt particular muscles and will strengthen the abdominals and back muscles.

WEIGHT MACHINE
It is possible to lift heavier weights on a machine. They are safer than free weights and do not require supervision. Some machines may be too large for smaller women. Add extra back/seat pads.

CROSS TRAINING

We have looked at six popular aerobic activities and the benefits each provide as an integral part of an active lifestyle. Many women will prefer to stick with a single activity and experience rapid improvements in fitness and health. Others may need more variety in their program to ensure their continuance. Cross training is the ideal way to achieve this.

Cross training is the combination of different activities to create an interesting and total body exercise program. It is a method that has long been used by competitive athletes who need to maintain fitness in the off-season, but who do not wish to train at their particular sport for various reasons.

With careful planning cross training can provide a more balanced program than a single activity because you can exercise all major muscle groups. For example, running strengthens the hamstring muscle group at the

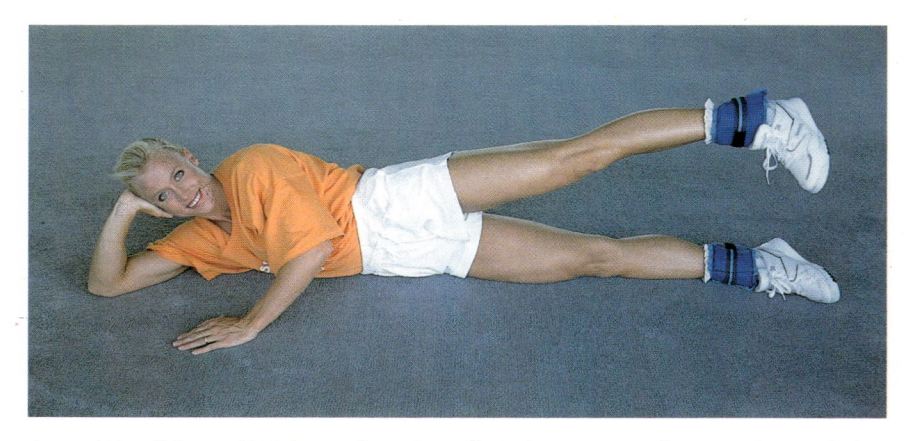

ANKLE, WRIST WEIGHTS Weights on the wrists will give your arms a better workout, which is good for toning because it increases muscular resistance. For weights on the ankles, use small, controlled movements. Leg exercises on the floor are non-impact exercises. It is wise not to jump, walk or run with ankle weights.

expense of the quadriceps; cycling strengthens the quadriceps more than the hamstrings. Including both activities in your program will ensure a balanced development of these muscle groups. Running and cycling develop the legs at the expense of the upper body, while swimming exercises the upper body at the expense of the lower body. A cross training program that includes running, cycling and swimming provides an optimum balance.

For these reasons cross training is perhaps the wisest choice for most people, other than those who wish to compete in a single sport.

Designing A Program

Irrespective of your age or current fitness level, some aerobic activity must be part of your plan. It should be scheduled on 3–5 days each week and last for at least 30 minutes.

You need to consider your fitness goals. If aerobic fitness is your primary goal, you will need to build up longer sessions. If it is strength development, then weight training will be your major activity. Aerobic dance may form the basis of a flexibility program. Refer back to the chart on page 83 for the benefits of the six aerobic activities.

Schedule your activities so that you alternate a hard day with an easy day or a rest day. The activity you perform on the hard day will probably be your primary activity.

EXAMPLE WEEKLY WORKOUT

Monday . . . . Walk 30-40 minutes
                    (including hills or soft sand)
Tuesday . . . . Aerobics or Weight Training
Wednesday . . Rest and Relaxation
Thursday . . . . Water workout, 30 minutes
Friday . . . . . . Cycle or Run or Squash, 30–40 minutes
Saturday . . . . Rest or Massage
Sunday . . . . . Long Bike Ride or Hike, 1–2 hours

Change your activities week by week and every now and then try something you've never done before. (Remember to include relaxation as part of your weekly program.)

Here is a list to give you some ideas: running, board riding, brisk walking, stair climbing, cycling, aerobics, hiking, weight training, swimming, body sculpting class, aqua-aerobics, stretch class, water skiing, relaxation, windsurfing, yoga, squash, circuit training, sex.

HOME WORKOUT

Exercising in the gym is an easy way to work out. It is social, fun and motivating. But there may be times when it is not possible to get to the gym because of work commitments, a young family, a new baby, bad weather, transport problems or finances.

Exercising at home can be just as beneficial. You will need a couple of items that help raise your heart rate, a well-ventilated open space, suitable flooring and some of your favourite music. The following items will help:

1 Exercise bike
2 Rebounder (small trampoline)
3 Skipping rope
4 Wrist or ankle weights (or fill socks with rice and tie at one end)
5 Dumbbells (or use cans of food)
6 Rubber band
7 Video on exercise

When you decide you are going to do a workout at home give yourself up to 45–60 minutes of undisturbed time. Plan what type of workout you are going to do and which body parts you want to reshape.

CROSS TRAINING

EXERCISE BIKE There are many types available for varying prices. Invest in one that suits your needs.

REBOUNDER This is great for warming up and for varied low-impact exercises. It is also good for lymphatic drainage.

SKIPPING ROPE Start off easily; skipping can increase your heart rate very quickly. Vary your steps and skip in an open space.

Select the appropriate exercises and be sure to perform them correctly for maximum benefit. Stretch each area of the body before and after exercise. An overworked muscle that isn't stretched will become sore the next day.

Depending on the intensity of your workout, your body will burn kilojoules for many hours afterwards. Exercising later in the day when your body starts to slow down is a good time.

Your workout should consist of the following:

DUMBBELLS Use for upper body toning. Don't hold too tightly; stay relaxed. Use a weight suitable for your strength. Using dumbbells that are too heavy may cause injury. Move the dumbbells in a controlled manner — do not let them swing.

RUBBER BANDS Always be careful to face away from the bands, as old or faulty bands could break. Stretch the band until it is taut, then pull from there. Keep tension high. It can be held in a variety of ways. Good for upper and lower body.

1. 5 minute warm up — e.g. stationary bike, easy jog until you feel a little sweaty

2. 5 minutes stretching — e.g. whole body stretches

3. 30 minutes aerobic with exercise — e.g. continuous exercise with heart rate between 60-80% of your maximum heart rate

If exercise becomes monotonous, work out a circuit, for example:

3 minute skips
3 minute sit-ups
3 minute walk around the house
20 half squats
5 push ups
20 bicep curls
20 tricep presses
TWICE

4. 10 minute cool down and stretching — e.g. easy on bike, slow walk around house. Finish off with 10 stretches and deep breathing

Concentrate on lengthening out worked muscles, deep breathe from the belly, close your eyes and think of something peaceful.

If you have a young child or baby with you, you'll be amazed how attentive they can be when you are doing lots of different moves. Encourage your child to join in where possible. (Keep babies away from bike wheels and dumbbells).

An additional benefit of home training is privacy. There is also no need to dress up, although do wear loose comfortable clothing.

EXERCISES TO AVOID

If you value your body don't ever do:
- Straight leg sit-ups
- Leg lowering on back
- Duck walks
- Back arching
- Locking up joints
- Bending head back

SKIP IT OFF!

Skipping is a great way to warm up for any exercise, but it can also be used as an exercise in itself. Skipping tones your muscles, especially your legs and arms. Depending on how fast you skip it can be good for your tummy as well. It also improves co-ordination, which is why boxers use it.

You need to work into skipping slowly as it can become quite strenuous. Start skipping as part of your exercise plan for 5 minutes, 3 times per week. Gradually increase the time per week by 2–3 minutes per session until you can skip 20–30 minutes, 3 times a week.

Choose a good surface to skip on. Wood floors, lowpile carpet or grass are the best surfaces. Do not skip on concrete as it offers no cushioning.

Wear shoes that are comfortable for aerobics or running. Skip in open spaces where you won't hit anything. Watch out for fans, pets and babies. If you intend skipping often, invest in a leather rope.

If you lose interest after five minutes put on your favourite music and skip to the beat.

Combine skipping with other aerobic activities — skip 5 minutes, walk quickly or jog around the house 3 times and repeat.

CROSS TRAINING

OVERTRAINING

You can train too hard. Often you will not really feel like training, you are tired and your body aches, but you still go and work out. Rest and relaxation are just as important to a healthy exercise program as the exercise itself.

To find out if you are overtraining, keep a record of your resting heart rate. Leave a notepad next to the bed and when you wake up in the morning take your heart rate over 60 seconds. If there is a marked increase, you may need more rest. This check can also tell you if you aren't 100% well. Watch for these symptoms of overtraining:

- fatigue
- insomnia
- muscle soreness
- depression
- irritability
- decreased athletic performance

Allow yourself plenty of rest and relaxation in between workouts. If you do become overtrained, you may need to cut back on your exercise until you feel refreshed again. Know your body and your limits, and know when to ease back.

CHAPTER EIGHT

MAINTAINING YOUR FITNESS PROGRAM

IT CAN BE DIFFICULT TO SUSTAIN YOUR MOTIVATION FOR EXERCISE. HOW DO YOU AVOID BECOMING AN EXERCISE DROPOUT?

It has been estimated that about 50% of people who begin a fitness and exercise program quit within six months. Each had good intentions when he or she began. The health benefits of exercise are generally well known. It can control weight, lower blood pressure, reduce the risk of heart disease and cancer and help prevent illness. Exercise enhances mental health, reduces stress and increases self-esteem. Even with all this in mind it is often difficult to stick with it. What is it that makes one person continue to exercise while another drops out?

The key to staying with exercise is to sustain your motivation. Here are a few suggestions to help you maintain your fitness for life.

Goals

A New Year's Resolution alone is not enough to motivate you. By February you will probably have become sidetracked and discouraged. Similarly, short-term motivation, such as a decision to lose 5 kilos in three months, will probably end in failure. You need to formulate long-term goals. To help you do this, write down your goals as suggested on page 18. Your decision to exercise regularly must be a deliberate one that you are fully committed to. This positive attitude will help you get out of bed early on that cold morning to exercise.

Plan

Exercise must be convenient enough for you to stay with it. Incorporate it into your daily and weekly plan as recommended on page 19. Have alternative exercises in case the weather is unfavourable. Don't join a gym that is too far away. Exercise close to home or work. If you are too tired after work, exercise in the morning. Enlist your family's support. If you prefer to exercise in the morning this may change the family's whole morning routine. You need to anticipate problems in advance and work out a plan together. If the evening is your preference, exercise immediately you get home. Don't mix that cocktail until you've completed your daily plan.

Pace

Start slowly and gradually build up over several weeks and months. It is no use writing '45 minute run' in your plan if you know you couldn't possibly do it. People who are overweight or in poor physical condition will experience pain or discomfort if they try to do too much too soon. This is discouraging and can lead to injury. Begin with a low-impact sport like walking or swimming and don't overdo it. If you are injured, scale down your exercise or change it to minimise the effect on the injured area, then gradually build up as the injury heals.

Progress

As already suggested, check your fitness level regularly and record the results. Complete your training log daily. Don't rely on the bathroom scales to monitor your progress. Within the first couple of days of regular exercise your body will begin to retain more fluid for the increased amount of sweating. You will also be adding muscle, which weighs more than fat. This is when the 'pinch' test can show you more positive changes in your body. Most importantly, be patient.

Boredom

You need to vary your exercise routine before boredom sets in. Incorporate cross training activities into your plan to provide variety. Change the route of your daily walk, or mix up a few laps of breaststroke or backstroke with freestyle in the pool. After a couple of months take up a new sport to provide a fresh challenge. Exercise with a friend or join a group program.

Commitment

Whatever you do, don't let anyone talk you out of what you have decided to achieve. Inevitably there will be plenty of people to tell you how ridiculous it all is. They will encourage you to be slack and try and convince you you'll never do it. Be ready for these negative attitudes. Some people knock others because they know they should be taking the positive steps themselves. Be firm in your resolve and mix with people who have similar goals.

Changes To Your Routine

Don't be discouraged if you must temporarily forego some of your exercise program. Changes in routine like a new job, a vacation, a business trip or a visitor invariably cause short-term setbacks. Maintain your fitness by an easy jog around the block or a brisk walk. While on holiday or away from home, climb the hotel stairs instead of taking the lift. This increases your heart rate, burns extra kilojoules and keeps muscles toned. When sightseeing, choose a walking tour rather than a bus tour. Plan a family holiday with some sort of activity involved.

Dropout Crises

If your motivation is low it is a good idea to temporarily stop your exercise program. It may suddenly have hit you that you will have to exercise like this for the rest of your life. Exercise has become a compulsion rather than a positive choice. A short break can help you refocus your goals. Your fitness level will drop during periods of inactivity but fortunately muscles have memory. Regaining lost fitness is usually easier than it was first time around.

Don't overburden yourself with guilt if you stop exercising. Examine why you stopped and attempt to tackle the situation. Because exercise helps relieve stress you will naturally become more anxious. Your appetite will also increase so monitor your kilojoule intake carefully. When you begin to retrain, start at a level lower than when you stopped. For example, don't take a full aerobics class the first time back, decrease the weights in your weight training program and run about half your usual kilometres.

Staying with your exercise program can seem a solitary struggle. But you are not alone. The pitfalls are universal and predictable. Once you have incorporated exercise into your lifestyle for 12 months, you will probably maintain your fitness for life.

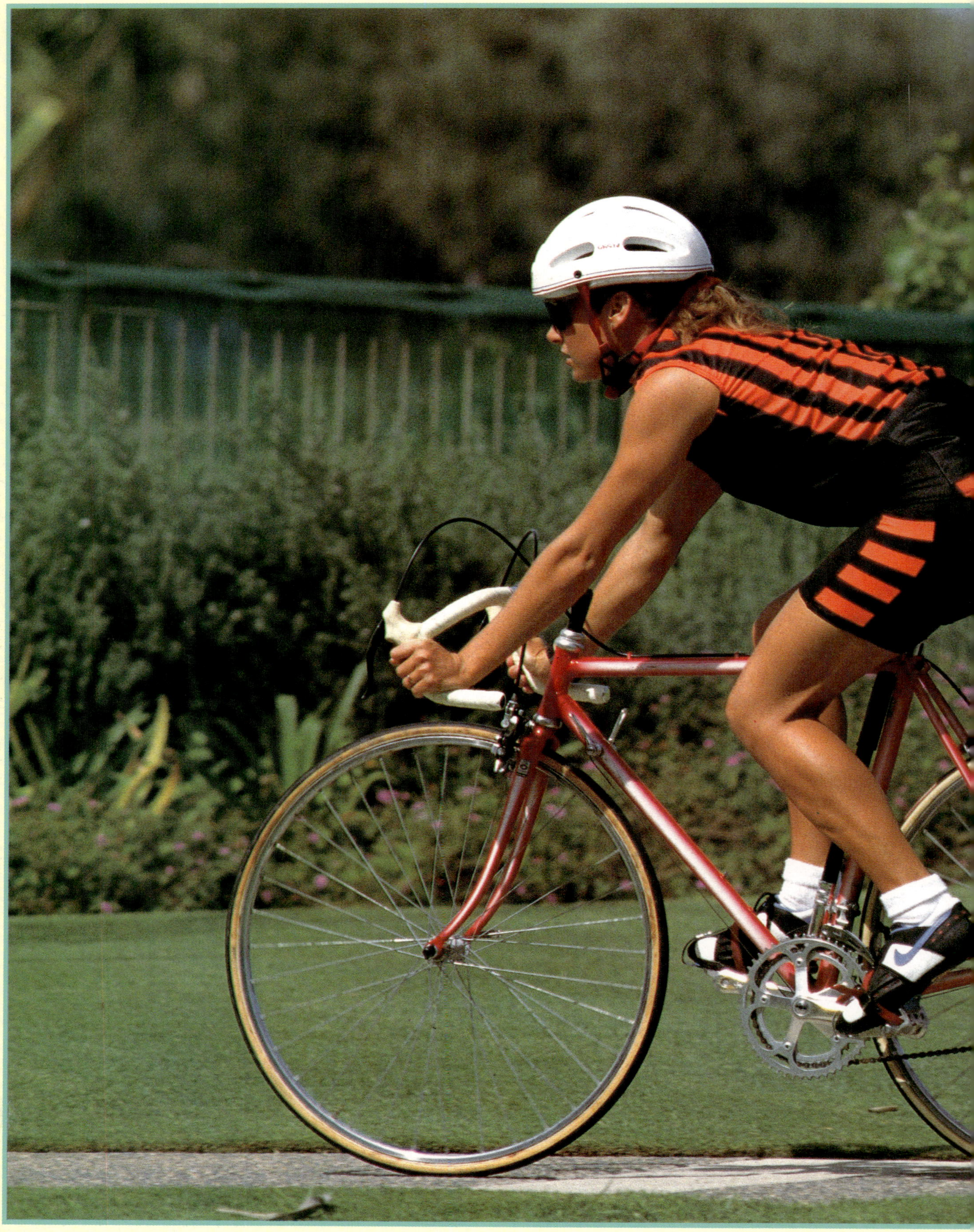

CHAPTER NINE

HEALTH AND SPORTS MEDICINE

LEARN TO RECOGNISE THE SYMPTOMS OF INJURY AND AIM TO PREVENT THEM

To avoid injury and maintain your body in peak condition it is a good idea to understand its intricate workings. All movement of the body is possible because of the combined action of muscles, tendons, ligaments, joints and bones.

Muscles are made up of long thin fibres arranged in bundles. They are thick in the middle (called the belly) and thin out at the ends where they form a tendon. The tendon attaches the muscle to the bone.

During activity muscles contract or shorten by one end remaining fixed (the origin) and the other end (the insertion) moving. Because the muscle tendons are attached to bone across joints, the unfixed end moves the bone at the joint. This is shown in the diagram where the biceps muscle contracts to flex or bend the elbow, while the triceps muscle contracts to extend or straighten the elbow. Muscles work in pairs, one to perform one movement, the other the opposite movement.

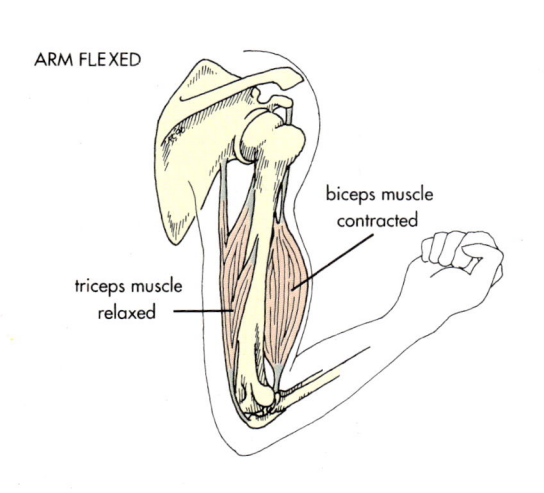

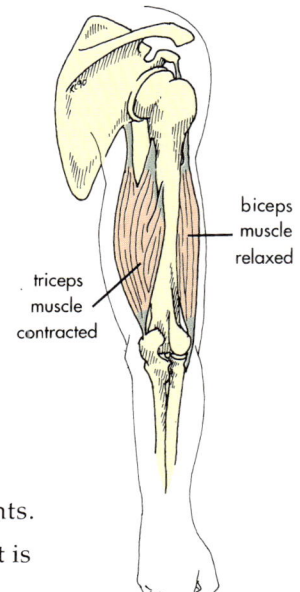

The movement described above occurs at joints. It is designed to permit a smooth action. A joint is formed when two (or more) bones meet and the structure is held together by ligaments. Ligaments also ensure that the movements are restricted to those for which the joint was designed. Ligaments are thick cord-like structures made up of tough fibres.

The joint most commonly injured during sports and exercise is the knee joint.

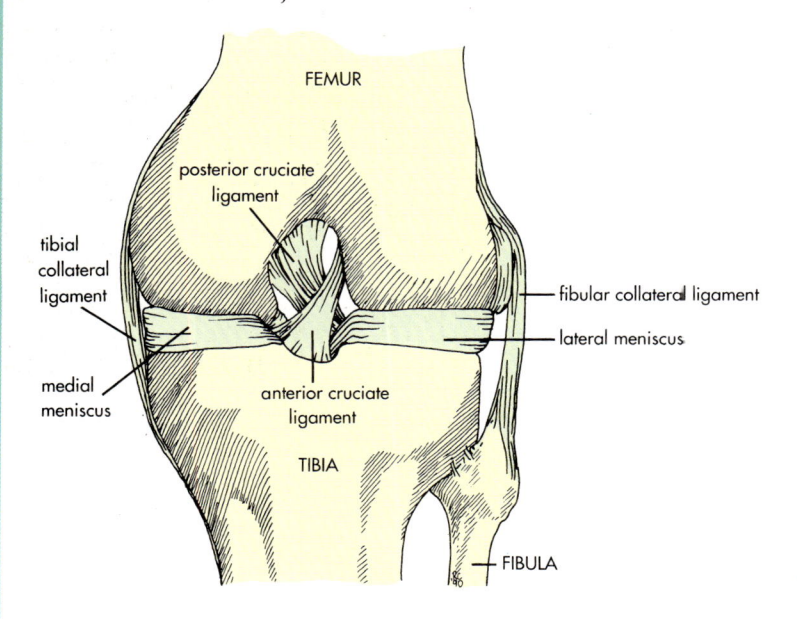

The integrity of the knee joint is maintained by the strength of the muscles and their tendons, and the ligaments that hold the long bones of the thigh (femur) and the shin (tibia) together. The ends of the bone are covered with cartilage and together with the menisci (found only in the knee joint) and joint fluid, allow the knee to flex and extend smoothly.

SOFT TISSUE INJURIES AND THEIR TREATMENT

The majority of exercise related injuries occur to one or more of the following tissues: muscles and tendons, ligaments, bones and joints. Injuries of this type are called soft tissue injuries.

The old adage 'no pain, no gain' is misleading for exercisers and athletes. Pain is a warning signal and may be related to several causes depending on its severity.

Following a good intense exercise session you may feel stiff and sore the next day. This is called delayed onset muscle soreness. It is normal, but working out day after day at an increased intensity may lead to injury. This is where you must know your body and your limits. Cut down on the intensity and rest if needed so that healing can take place and injury won't occur.

Generally the immediate treatment for all soft tissue injuries is the same, and is called the RICE procedure:

- **R** rest the injured part
- **I** ice is applied to the injured part
- **C** compression (or pressure) is applied
- **E** elevation of the injured part

The treatment should be continued for at least 20 minutes, and as soon after injury as possible. The application of ice reduces blood flow into the injured area and thus reduces swelling. (The immediate application of heat or massage will increase swelling and the injury will take longer to heal). The RICE treatment should continue long enough for the injured part to become numb. During this time some light movements or stretching should be done. The procedure can be continued for up to seven days.

If the pain is severe, to the point where lifting the limb affected is difficult, the injury may need other treatment. If the injury does not respond to the RICE treatment, seek the advice of a qualified health professional such as a medical practitioner familiar with sports medicine procedures, or a physiotherapist. The Australian Sports Medicine Federation has branches in all states (see appendix) and will supply you with the names of suitable professionals near you.

Muscle and Tendon Injuries

The muscle groups most commonly injured are the quadriceps and hamstrings. The injury usually takes the form of a strain or tear and occurs as a result of insufficient warm-up prior to rapid acceleration such as in a sprint.

Injuries to tendons are commonly seen in the elbow (tennis elbow), shoulder (swimmers' shoulder) and ankle (Achilles tendon). They are often associated with overuse problems. They require complete rest from the activity causing the problem. Prevention is the key to handling these injuries. You should develop the strength of the muscles involved in the relevant movement, maintain a high level of flexibility and always use the correct technique during the performance of the skill.

Muscle stiffness following exercise is believed to be caused by minute muscle tears. A muscle is torn when it is lengthened rather than the more common movement of shortening. An example would

TREAT YOURSELF NATURALLY

If you are feeling unwell, don't head for medication straight away. Drugs may take away the symptoms but they will not necessarily take away the cause of the ailment. Learn to recognise the symptoms of illness and aim to prevent them. If you are sick, nauseous or headachey, you may be overstressed, overtired or your diet may be unbalanced. The dangerous long-term side effects of headache pills, relaxation drugs and stimulants are enough cause for you to seek an alternative solution. Learn to listen to your body and realise that problems like lethargy, lack of motivation and pre-menstrual blues have a logical cause.

be the lengthening of the quadriceps while running downhill or walking down a flight of stairs. This type of muscle contraction is called eccentric and is common in exercise and sport situations. If you experience muscle soreness take it as a signal to have either a rest day or a fairly light workout.

LIGAMENT INJURIES

These are called sprains. They range from minor, requiring minimum rehabilitation time, to major, requiring surgery and a long rehabilitation period. The most common injury is to the ligaments of the outer side of the ankle joint. This could be caused by stepping in a hole or landing on the side of the foot in netball. In sports that require many sudden changes of direction, such as aerobics or squash, injuries to the knee are quite common. These injuries often involve the medial ligament, or if more severe the cruciate ligament. Injuries of this type require professional advice for diagnosis and rehabilitation. Strengthening of the muscles which operate the knee joint (i.e., the quadriceps and hamstrings) helps prevent this injury.

BONE AND JOINT INJURIES

A fairly common problem experienced by those beginning exercise, particularly running, is shin soreness. This is generally caused by a number of factors including running too much too soon (either distance or speed), an overweight condition, and inappropriate footwear for the type of exercise performed. If injury persists it is advisable to seek the advice of a suitable health professional early to ensure a speedy recovery.

HEAT INJURY

We need to be aware of the dangers of exercise in the harsh Australian climate. While women generally have a better control of heat regulation than males (because they have more fat tissue) care still needs to be taken when exercising in hot environmental temperatures.

Once the body loses 3% of its weight in fluid it will fatigue more easily. This is because the fluid from sweat comes from the blood and tissues and therefore a drop in their water content means they do not function as efficiently. If the deficit falls below 5% then the exerciser is in danger of serious heat injury, as sweat is the basis of the body's cooling system.

This situation can occur fairly easily in endurance activities, such as running, if the athlete does not drink sufficient water before (approximately 500 mls) and during the run (250 mls every 15 minutes). Thirst is not a good indicator of the body's need for water. By the time you feel thirsty you have been in need of water for some time.

Electrolyte replacement drinks should not be taken during exercise. Their high salt content makes dehydration worse. Instead they should be taken at the end of the workout in a very dilute solution.

OTHER INJURIES

Cramps This common muscular problem usually occurs as a result of fatigue and/or low levels of some minerals, notably sodium and potassium, or from a circulatory impairment, which reduces blood flow and therefore oxygen supply to a muscle. Relief can be obtained by gentle stretching of the affected muscle in a rested state and the restoration of the minerals lost by taking an electrolyte replacement drink.

Stitch This occurs as a cramp-like pain that affects the side, just under the ribs, during exercise. The most likely cause is an irregular or incorrect breathing technique leading to lack of oxygen in either the diaphragm or the muscles between the ribs. If it occurs, stretch the arm on the affected side as high as possible, or bend the trunk forwards. Pressing your fingers into the affected area while exhaling can also give some relief. If the condition persists it may be wise to check with your doctor to ensure that no underlying abdominal problem exists.

Blisters These are caused by friction with shoes or equipment. This produces a separation of skin layers, thus allowing fluid to accumulate between them. If the blister is large (greater than 1 cm in diameter) or is painful, it may be necessary to drain it. Prevent blisters on the feet by wearing properly fitting shoes, or by wearing two pairs of socks, particularly if your feet perspire excessively.

Swimmer's Ear (Otitis externa) This is a bacterial infection of the ear caused by water being trapped in the ear canal. Sufferers experience itching and pain and even a partial hearing loss. It may or may not be accompanied by a discharge. If left untreated the infection may spread to the middle ear and cause disruption of balance. Prevent it by ensuring that the ear canal is thoroughly dried after each swim. Using ear drops with a 1–3% boric acid solution will also help prevent infection.

Eye Irritations These were once a common source of annoyance for swimmers. If you wear goggles when you swim you should have no problem. If your eyes do become irritated wash them out with ordinary tap water.

SPECIAL SITUATIONS

Menstruation and Exercise At the elite level of female participation in sports the phases of the menstrual cycle do not seem to have a bearing on the quality of performance. This is not to say that the ability of some women to participate in exercise and sports is not affected by dysmenorrhea (painful periods) or pre-menstrual tension. Research into the relationship between menstruation and exercise needs to be extended. There is some evidence to suggest that exercise can be used as a preventive measure for dysmenorrhea.

Heavy training (e.g. running in excess of 160 km per week) may induce amenorrhea (cessation of periods). The long-term effects of this also need to be more fully researched, but it is known that it can cause a reduction in bone density. Most athletes resume menstruation when the training intensity is decreased.

As iron is lost during menstruation, it must be replaced in menstruating athletes. If the iron store becomes depleted anaemia results and performance will drop. Because only a relatively small proportion of the iron in food is able to be absorbed in the intestine, women who exercise may need to consider iron supplementation. Check with your medical practitioner before doing this as supplementation of an already high iron level can be dangerous.

Exercise can be safely continued throughout pregnancy, but expectant mothers should take care not to exercise in the heat of the day.

Pregnancy and Exercise Historically, one of the strongest arguments against the participation of women in sports, particularly endurance activities, has been related to the erroneous idea that it will injure the reproductive organs. Similar arguments have been put forward against pregnant women exercising, particularly with the added possibility of injury to, or spontaneous abortion of the developing foetus.

Exercise, even strenuous activity, can be continued throughout pregnancy with safety. The form of exercise may need to be adapted in the later months to accommodate the change in physical size. There is sufficient evidence available to be able to say with confidence that there is no need for women to cease exercise during or after their pregnancy. The baby is well protected in the bony pelvis and does not suffer physically or physiologically from its mother's activity. The improved well-being and other psychological benefits to the mother make exercise worthwhile.

One aspect that may pose a potential risk, however, is that of heat injury. For this reason the expectant mother should avoid exercise in very hot environmental conditions. In normal conditions she should take care to maintain an adequate level of hydration as recommended above.

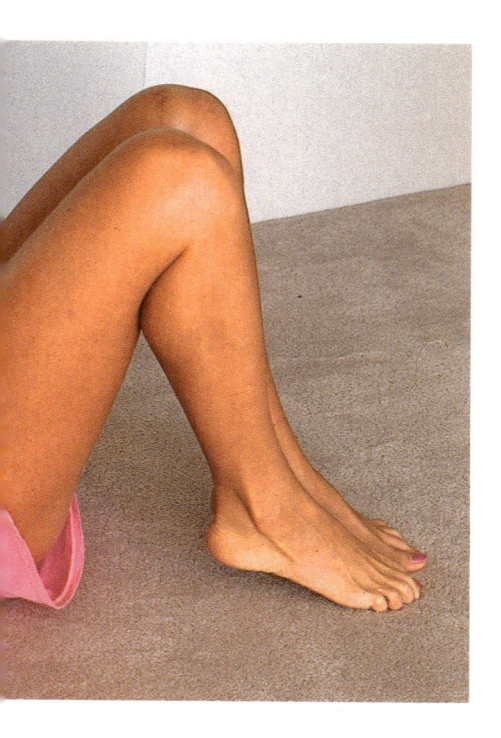

There is some evidence to suggest that various women have produced their best athletic performances following childbirth. This implies that bearing children may confer some hitherto unknown physiological benefit. However, this needs further research for clarification.

The woman who wants to continue her exercise program into her pregnancy has no need to fear complications as a direct result of exercise. Any complications will be those already present. It is wise to maintain regular checks with your doctor so that he or she may detect any problems early and give advice.

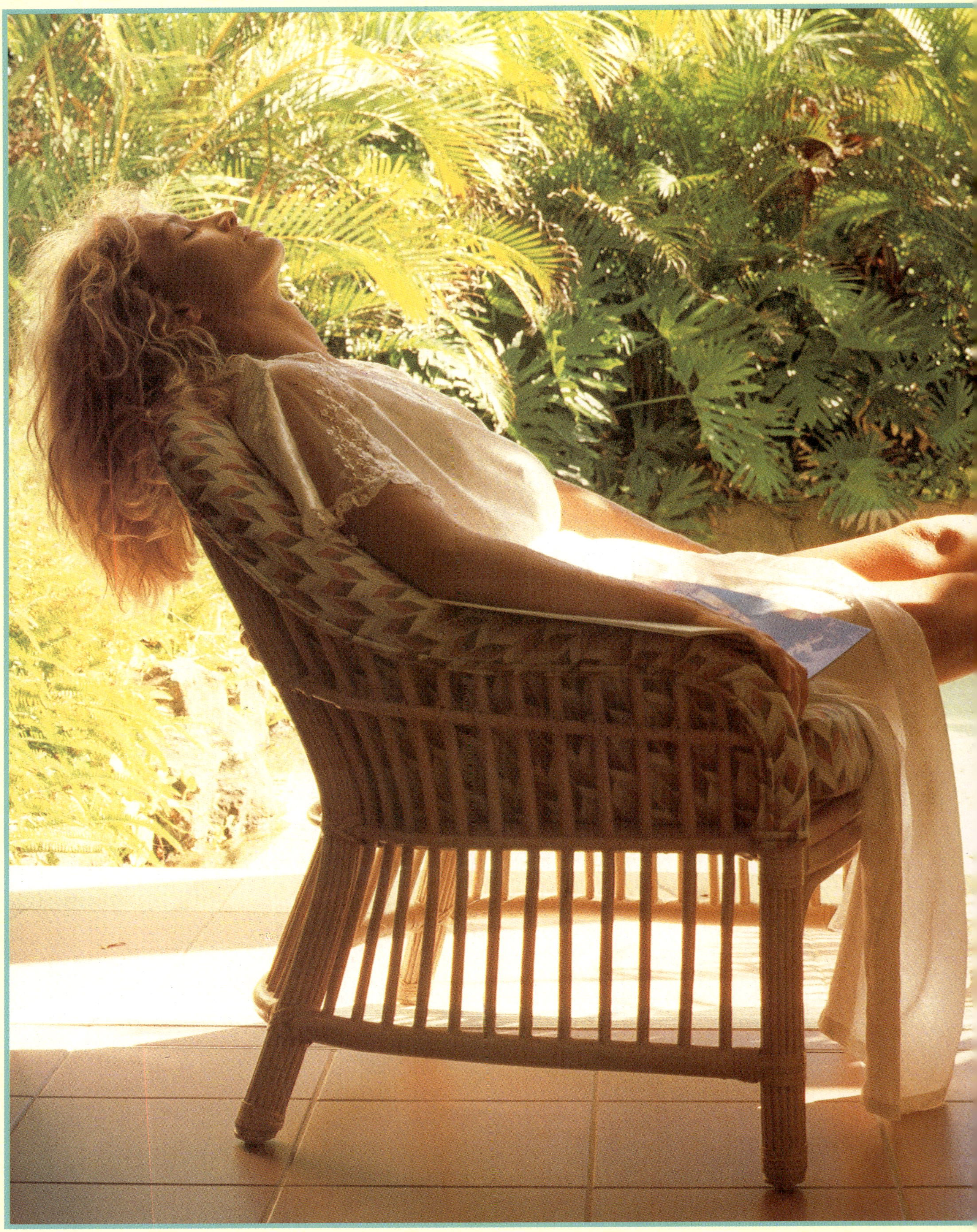

CHAPTER TEN

THERE'S MORE TO LIFE THAN EXERCISE

HAVING TIME FOR YOURSELF WILL HELP YOU FEEL REVITALISED, CONFIDENT AND ENERGETIC

Whatever your profession may be — whether you work at home caring for children, full time or part time in the outside workforce, married mother, single mother, school, college or university student, attached or unattached — you still need time for yourself. One of the most important aspects of living a fulfilled and happy life is to take time off to do something that you enjoy.

Everyone needs a release from the constant demands they are faced with. It isn't easy working full time and looking a family. When you take time out for yourself, you will find that whatever or whoever you go back to will be grateful for your renewed enthusiasm. More importantly, you will feel revitalised, confident and energetic.

Whatever your budget, you need to find a way to pamper yourself. Put your family and work commitments on hold every so often (they will still be there when you come home). Try some things that relax your body — have a massage, facial or manicure, or experiment with a new hairstyle. Maybe your idea of pampering yourself is to do absolutely nothing. Whatever it is that you fantasise about, go and do it.

Try not to feel that you are neglecting your 'commitments'. At first you may feel guilty pampering yourself, but it really is the best way to feel revitalised. Here are some suggestions for you to try.

HEAT THERAPY AND WATER THERAPY

Warmth and water are two of the greatest comforts known to the human body. The foetus develops in a warm, fluid environment and we naturally associate these mediums with a sense of security and well-being. If you live near a beach, warmth and water will be an inexpensive luxury. There is nothing quite as relaxing as lying on warm sand under the early morning sun and refreshing yourself every now and again in the cool ocean.

For those not so fortunate as to live near the beach there are some equally relaxing therapies you can partake in such as spa baths, saunas, steam baths and so on. The Russian bath is a steam-filled sauna. The benefits are immediate — a glowing complexion, easier respiration, relaxed muscles and a general sense of well-being.

Some therapies involve dry heat. This produces a temporary situation in the body where the blood vessels dilate, the body temperature rises slightly and there is an increased blood supply to the area being treated. This

There's More to Life Than Exercise

brings relief to musculo-skeletal conditions such as arthritis, rheumatism and sciatica.

Hydrotherapy or the bubbling spa is an ancient remedy popular in Roman times. Today spa baths are to be found in health clubs and many private homes. Hydrotherapy is recommended for all kinds of bodily complaints, ranging from aching muscles and tired skin, to chronic joint and bone conditions. The bubbling water jets create an underwater massage that can be directed to any part of the body. Because the body is weightless in water and the muscles are relaxed, the effects of the massage are far reaching.

If you do not have access to a spa bath, packs or compressors can be used as an alternative. Although this does not produce a massaging effect, hot cloths soaked in water and placed on the skin dilate the blood vessels. Alternatively, cold packs can be used to reduce congestion or swelling.

Be sure to drink lots of water before, during and after any kind of heat treatment. Mineral water is often drunk for the reputed health benefits of its mineral content. The gaseous form is believed to be easier for the body to assimilate.

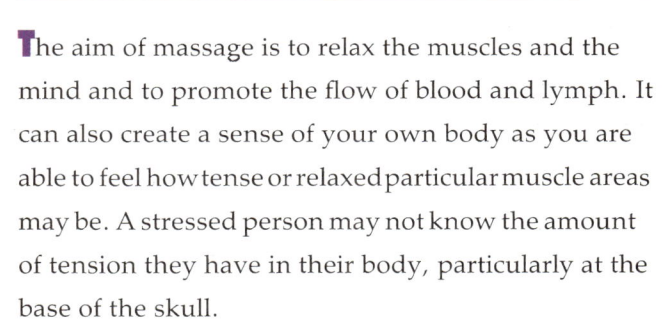

MASSAGE

The aim of massage is to relax the muscles and the mind and to promote the flow of blood and lymph. It can also create a sense of your own body as you are able to feel how tense or relaxed particular muscle areas may be. A stressed person may not know the amount of tension they have in their body, particularly at the base of the skull.

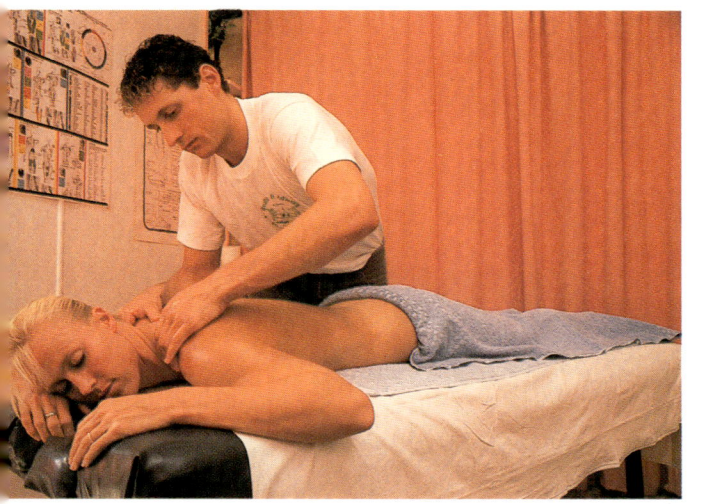

Depending on your needs, you can seek out a professional, or be massaged by a friend or partner. If you require a professional it is a good idea to make enquiries at your local health club. Avoid newspaper advertisements, these can be a risk at times. Perhaps you and your partner could take a massage course.

Not only is massage a source of pleasure, it also improves circulation, relieves pain and promotes relaxation. The sequence of massage is purely up to the individual. It is usual to start on the back, then shoulders, neck, buttocks, thighs and legs. Turn over and continue with the arms, hands, head and face, the front of the shoulders, the stomach, legs, ankles and feet.

THE ALEXANDER TECHNIQUE

Your posture, the way you sit and stand every day, can have a marked effect on your health, mental alertness and general sense of well-being. Years of incorrect posture, such as slouching in an armchair, can have both physical and emotional effects.

Massage is a wonderful way to relax. It also helps circulation and relieves 'tension knots'.

The Alexander Technique aims to correct bad posture habits. It can only be taught by a qualified person. It is a gradual re-education of the body's positioning. After correction, one can actually 'grow' a few centimetres taller. To learn the technique you would need to spend about 30 sessions with an instructor. Here is a simple exercise to give you an idea. Stand with your lower back against a wall, knees bent, head slightly inclined forward. If you find this tiring you may need to correct your posture. Slowly straighten your knees and feel how your stance has changed.

While reading about the Alexander Technique you probably sat up a little straighter in your chair, something we were told to do at primary school.

At school many of us ended up over-arching our backs, this is also wrong. The spine has natural curves that need to be catered for. To sit correctly one must have both feet firmly on the floor, eyes level and the back naturally straight.

New chairs have been developed to incorporate the natural position of the spine and legs. They are commonly known as kneeling chairs. The weight is carried by the bottom and part of the knees. The angle of the hip joint is much wider than the usual 90 per cent.

The most common habit of bad posture is for the head to be tilted forwards so the chin juts out in front. Another complication is a severely arched neck caused by pulling the head back to correct the forward incline of the neck.

By seeking professional advice to correct your posture, you can eliminate these bad habits and at the same time enjoy a heightened sense of physical and emotional well-being.

OTHER TREATMENTS

Some other treatments for your body include yoga, acupuncture, osteopathy and chiropractic. All have been shown to have benefits to the individual, although most are still regarded as alternative treatments.

Yoga, once learned, can be practised alone. It offers people of all ages and all levels of fitness improved physical flexibility, freedom from stress and a profound sense of well-being. It concentrates on breathing and body positioning, using one's full mental focus and attention. Traditional yoga teaches harmony of the body, mind and spirit.

Acupuncture is an ancient Chinese therapy used not only to treat sickness, but to maintain the body in the best health. It is used on particular areas of the body surface, which are said to relate to internal organs. Fine needles are inserted into the skin at these particular points. It is believed that this stimulates blocked energy. Doctors of western medicine are beginning to incorporate acupuncture as part of their treatments, at times instead of medication.

Osteopathy and chiropractic are treatment methods related to the back, or more precisely, the spine. It is thought that 80% of Australians suffer from back pain at some time. Osteopathy is a practice arising from misuse of the bones and joints of the spine and treats the mechanical disorders related to the spine.

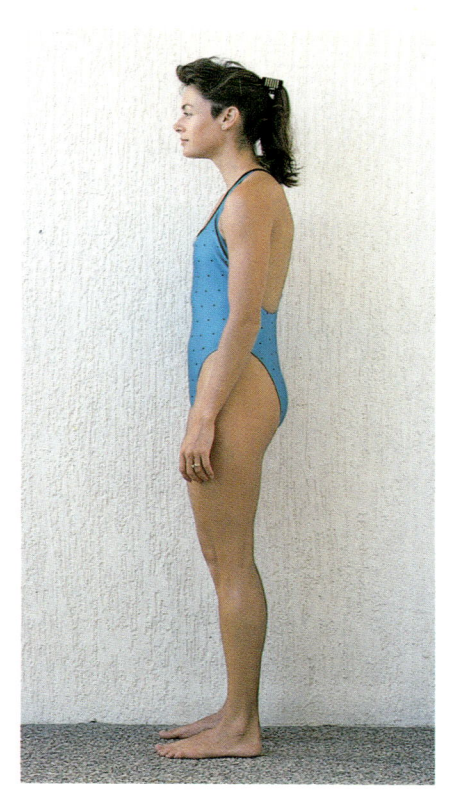

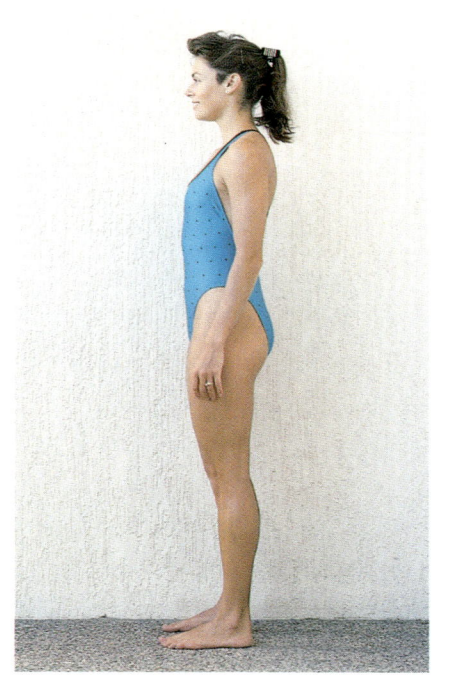

Bad posture (top) can be corrected (above) by the Alexander Technique, which re-educates the body's positioning.

An osteopathic lesion may be a muscle spasm, an irritated nerve manifested as a sprain, strain, swelling or similar. The spinal cord is the link between the brain and the body. Spinal nerves arise from the spinal cord and spread to different parts of the body. The spinal cord also administers the autonomic nervous system, which includes the respiratory, digestive, circulatory and other functions. If the back is put out by such things as lifting, the osteopath can give immediate relief.

Chiropractic treatment is usually more popular than osteopathy. It is similar in concept and widely used for injuries as well as prevention. It is believed that if the spine is just very slightly out of alignment (known as subluxation), the whole bodily system can be affected. Chiropractic diagnosis is similar to osteopathic but makes more use of x-rays and blood, urine and neurological tests. Be sure to seek out a trained and qualified chiropractor for your own protection.

SELF-ENHANCEMENT

As well as seeking out the treatments above, many people may want to find other ways to enhance themselves. You may want to pay attention to some things you can change about yourself — your skin, hair, nails and teeth.

Your skin takes good care of itself. Although we feel refreshed after a good bath we often dry out our skin with too much soap. Be sure to relubricate the skin with moisturiser. Treat yourself to a facial every now and then. This provides a thorough cleansing as well as a massage to increase circulation. The sun is the biggest danger to your skin. Never put your face in the sun. Always wear a hat and 15$^+$SPF sunscreen. Even with this protection UV rays will

Pamper yourself by having a facial. It is relaxing and thoroughly cleanses your skin.

reach your face. Avoid exposure to the sun during the middle hours of the day. Smoking also ages the skin.

Wrapping yourself in scented oils and herbs just for a treat can be marvellous for the pores of your skin. Ask at your health club or beauty salon. Remember not to wear perfume when sunbathing. Some perfumes can cause unpleasant reactions in sunlight.

Changing your hairstyle can give you a great psychological lift and make you feel pampered. Choose a style that suits your lifestyle. If you're always on the go you need something quick and manageable.

Nails are actually tough, dead material called keratin, but they are directly related to our state of health. These dead cells grow from a root near the base of the nail where the cells divide rapidly. Blood vessels in the soft tissue beneath the nail nourish the nail bed, which is visible as a white crescent. Most nail problems are

Sunscreen is especially important in the harsh Australian sun.

Sunscreen should always be complemented by a sun hat.

not caused by dietary deficiencies as commonly believed, but by abuse and lack of care. Treat yourself to a manicure every so often and look after your hands. If you suffer from stiff fingers, exercise them as much as possible.

The old myth that an apple cleans your teeth after a meal is false. It may be an abrasive, but the harmful bacteria usually sits in between the teeth and gums and needs careful brushing and flossing. A six-monthly visit to the dentist may not be your idea of pampering yourself, but a beautiful smile is worth it. Cutting down on foods that are high in sugar makes looking after your teeth a lot easier.

There are of course many other ways to pamper yourself. You need to decide what gives you pleasure and organise some regular time to indulge in it. The resulting benefit to your whole health will make your life more enjoyable and fun.

STANDING POSTURE

To achieve correct body alignment when standing, the following parts of your body should be in a straight line:
- ear hole
- shoulder (tip of the acromium process)
- hip (behind the hip joint)
- knee (through the middle of the knee joint)
- ankle (in front of the ankle joint)

WALKING POSTURE

In walking there should be no wasted motion in the side-to-side or lateral plane. The motion of the arms and legs should be limited and the trunk movement minimal.
- legs should swing forward from the hip, with the heel striking the ground first
- the feet should be straight ahead
- the body weight should pass over the outer border of the foot to the ball of the foot
- the arms should swing freely without rigidity
- the abdomen should be uplifted, the spine extended and the chest expanded

Some common faults in walking posture are:
- leaning forward or backward before the foot strikes the ground
- an exaggerated shift of weight to support the foot
- swinging arms too wide
- failure to swing arms

I hope that you have learnt some valuable information reading this book. I know I certainly have researching it.

Fitness is possible for everyone — the young, the old, males or females. It may seem an impossible goal at times, but when I trained for the 1990 Commonwealth Games, I discovered that if you feel committed, there is no limit to what you can achieve. Believe in yourself!

Learn from reading, learn from others and pass on what you have learnt to your partner, friends, family, and most importantly, to your children. Help them to have a full and healthy life.

When I travel around Australia on promotional tours, my advice to people is always the same:

- enjoy what you are doing
- be self-confident
- laugh often
- remember the simple things
- money means nothing without health and happiness
- strive for excellence
- be enthusiastic

But most importantly . . . have fun.

Lisa Curry

APPENDICES A TO E

APPENDIX A

PHYSICAL ACTIVITY READINESS QUESTIONNAIRE (PAR-Q)
A self-administered questionnaire for adults

PAR-Q is designed to help you help yourself. Many health benefits are associated with regular exercise, and the completion of PAR-Q is a sensible first step to take if you are planning to increase the amount of physical activity in your life.

For most people physical activity should not pose any problem or hazard. PAR-Q has been designed to identify the small number of adults for whom physical activity might be inappropriate or those who should have medical advice concerning the type of activity most suitable for them.

Common sense is your best guide to answering these few questions. Please read them carefully and tick the yes or no opposite the question if it applies to you.

YES NO

1. Has your doctor ever said you have heart trouble?
2. Do you frequently have pains in your heart and chest?
3. Do you often feel faint or have spells of severe dizziness?
4. Has a doctor ever said your blood pressure was too high?
5. Has your doctor ever told you that you have a bone or joint problem such as arthritis that has been aggravated by exercise, or might be made worse with exercise?
6. Is there a good physical reason not mentioned here why you should not follow an activity program even if you wanted to?
7. Are you over age 65 and not accustomed to vigorous exercise?

If you answered YES to one or more questions:

If you have not recently done so, consult with your doctor by telephone or in person before increasing your physical activity and/or taking a fitness test. Tell them what questions you answered yes on PAR-Q, or show them your copy.

After medical evaluation, seek advice from your doctor as to your suitability for:

- unrestricted physical activity, probably on a gradually increasing basis
- restricted or supervised activity to meet your specific needs, at least initially. Check in your community for special programs or services.

If you answered NO to all questions and as long as you answered PAR-Q accurately, you should be able to undertake:

- a graduated exercise program. A gradual increase in proper exercise promotes good fitness development while minimising or eliminating discomfort.
- an exercise test. Simple tests of fitness or more complex types may be undertaken if you so desire.

Postpone the above if you have a temporary illness, such as a common cold.

Produced by the British Columbia Ministry of Health.

TRAINING LOG

DAY	DATE	TIME	ACTIVITY	RESTING HEART RATE	EXERCISE HEART RATE	DISTANCE – KMS TIME – HRS	COMMENTS: e.g. body response, emotional feelings, weather, health, training program, massage, relaxation, intensity of workout (low mod high)
M							
T							
W							
T							
F							
S							
S							
WEEK NO.						WEEK'S TOTAL	HAVE YOU ACHIEVED YOUR WEEKLY GOAL? GOALS FOR NEXT WEEK?

EXAMPLE

TRAINING LOG

DAY	DATE	TIME	ACTIVITY	RESTING HEART RATE	EXERCISE HEART RATE	DISTANCE – KMS TIME – HRS	COMMENTS: e.g. body response, emotional feelings, weather, health, training program, massage, relaxation, intensity of workout (low mod high)
M	8/10	6.30 AM / 2.30 PM	WALK / WALK	65	138 / 140	40 MINS / 30 MINS	FIRST DAY – FELT GOOD. GOT O.K. FROM DOCTOR. ENJOYED WALK WITH KIDS FROM SCHOOL
T	9/10	9.30 – 10.30	AEROBICS CLASS	64	162	60 MINS	FELT GOOD – LEGS A LITTLE TIRED FROM WALKING YESTERDAY. WORKED ON BREATHING DURING CLASS
W	10/10	12 – 2	FACIAL MANICURE	65	—	2 HRS	LOVELY DAY
T	11/10	7 – 8	SWIM	66	160	1 KM (60 MINS) (20 LAPS)	VERY REFRESHING, MUST TAKE MY FRIEND AND INVEST IN SWIM SUIT. OUT FOR DINNER – VERY HEALTHY
F	12/10	9.30 – 10.30	AEROBICS CLASS + CIRCUIT	66	164	90 MINS	CIRCUIT WAS FUN – BIT HOT, REMEMBER MY WATER BOTTLE

WEIGHT SKINFOLD GRAPH

WEIGHT	WEEK 1	WEEK 2	WEEK 3	WEEK 4	WEEK 5	WEEK 6	WEEK 7	WEEK 8	WEEK 9	WEEK 10	WEEK 11	WEEK 12	SKINFOLDS
(kg)													(mm)
70													150
69													145
68													140
67													135
66													130
65													125
64													120
63													115
62													110
61													105
60													100
59													95
58													90
57													85
56													80
55													75
54													70
53													65
52													60
51													55
50													50
WEIGHT	1	2	3	4	5	6	7	8	9	10	11	12	SKINFOLDS

EXAMPLE

WEIGHT SKINFOLD GRAPH

WEIGHT	WEEK 1	WEEK 2	WEEK 3	WEEK 4	WEEK 5	WEEK 6	WEEK 7	WEEK 8	WEEK 9	WEEK 10	WEEK 11	WEEK 12	SKINFOLDS
(kg)													(mm)
70													150
69													145
68	X W												140
67													135
66		X	X										130
65													125
64	X S	X											120
63													115
62			X										110
61													105

FITNESS TEST RESULTS

ITEM	INITIAL SCORE	RATING	1	2	3	4	5	6	7	8	9	10
DATE												
WEIGHT	kg											
CLOTHING SIZE												
GIRTHS:												
Biceps	cm											
Waist	cm											
Thigh	cm											
Calf	cm											
SKINFOLDS:												
Triceps	mm											
Biceps	mm											
Shoulder	mm											
Abdomen	mm											
Hip	mm											
Thigh	mm											
Calf	mm											
Axilla	mm											
Sum	mm											
HEART RATE:												
Resting	bpm											
Maximum	bpm											
Training	bpm											
AEROBIC FITNESS:												
VO_2 max	ml kg min											
Step test	bpm											
12-min run	m											
12-min cycle	m											
12-min swim	m											
ABDOMINAL STRENGTH:												
Score												
FLEXIBILITY:												
Score	cm											

APPENDIX B

TESTS OF FITNESS
Body Composition

The following sites are used for measurement of skinfolds and are the same as those used in the assessment of athletes at the Australian Institute of Sport (Telford et al, 1966).

- **Triceps:** midway between the acromion and olecranon processes on the posterior aspect of the arm, the arm held vertically with the fold running parallel to the length of the arm.
- **Subscapular:** a fold running downward and laterally at about 30 from the vertical. 1 cm below the inferior angle of the scapula.
- **Suprailiac:** 4 cm above the anterior superior iliac spine the fold parallel to the fibres of the external oblique muscle.
- **Abdomen:** vertical fold adjacent to the umbilicus.
- **Biceps:** midway between the acromion process and the antecupital space.
- **Axilla:** on the mid-axillary line at the level of the xiphoid process. Subject's hand placed on head.
- **Thigh:** on anterior midline half-way from anterior superior iliac spine to top of patella.
- **Calf:** subject seated lower leg vertical. Fold at greatest circumference taken medially and vertically.

The measurements at each site are then added to give a sum of skinfolds in millimetres from the table below. Ascertain your rating for your age group.

Note: Record your weight and skinfold measurements on page 160 or photocopy and attach to your training log.

RATING	<35 (mm) (FEMALES)	>35 (mm) (FEMALES)	<35 (mm) (MALES)	>35 (mm) (MALES)
6	<70	<80	<50	<60
5	71–90	81–100	51–70	61–80
4	91–110	101–120	71–90	81–100
3	111–130	121–140	91–110	101–120
2	131–150	141–160	111–130	121–140
1	>150	>160	>130	>140

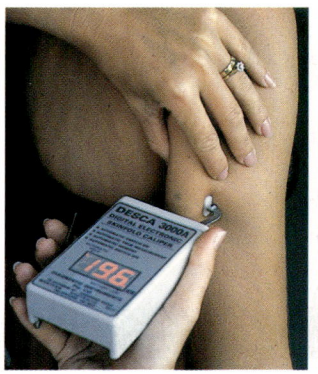

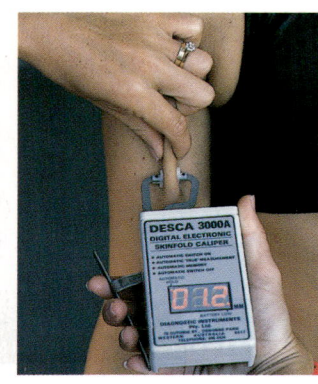

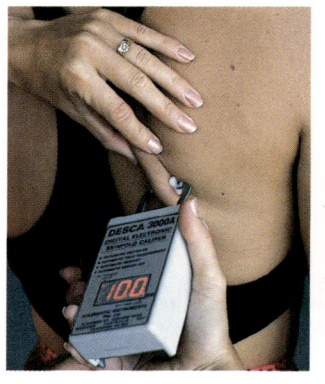

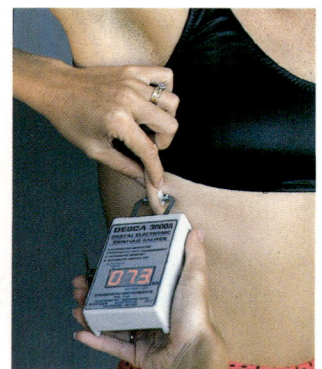

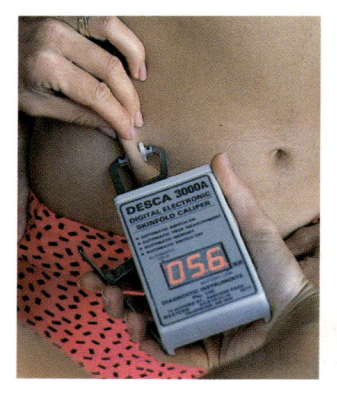

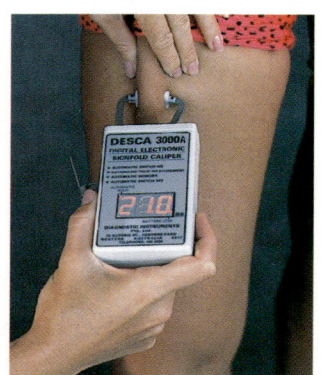

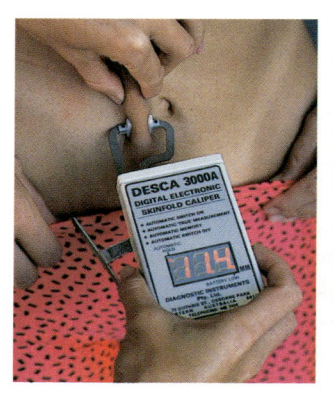

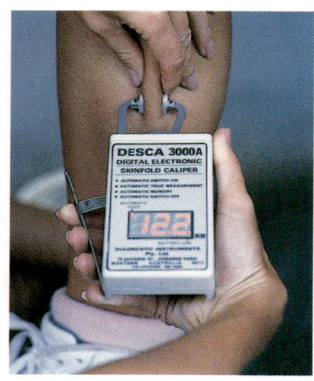

AEROBIC FITNESS

Test of Maximal Oxygen Consumption (VO₂ max)

- direct measurement (tested in Work Performance Laboratory)
- indirect measurement (based on the Astrand Submaximal Cycle Ergometer Test)

RATINGS: MAXIMAL OXYGEN UPTAKE (VO_2 max):

RATING (FEMALES)	20–29 (ML/KG/MIN)	30–39 (ML/KG/MIN)	40–49 (ML/KG/MIN)	50–59 (ML/KG/MIN)	>60 (ML/KG/MIN)
6	>55	>49	>45	>41	<38
5	48–54	44–48	41–44	36–40	34–37
4	43–47	38–43	36–40	31–35	28–33
3	36–42	32–37	30–35	27–30	23–27
2	31–35	25–31	24–29	23–26	19–22
1	<30	<24	<23	<22	<18

RATING (MALES)	20–29 (ML/KG/MIN)	30–39 (ML/KG/MIN)	40–49 (ML/KG/MIN)	50–59 (ML/KG/MIN)	>60 (ML/KG/MIN)
6	>65	>58	>50	>46	>42
5	58–64	50–57	43–49	39–45	35–41
4	52–57	43–49	37–42	33–38	29–34
3	44–51	37–42	33–36	27–32	24–28
2	36–43	31–36	29–32	23–26	21–23
1	<35	<30	<28	<22	<20

STEP TEST

This test is based on the principle that the better the fitness, the lower is the heart rate after a standard exercise.

Equipment   stop watch
33 cm high (12 inches) bench

Procedure

- step up right foot then left, then down right then down left — this counts one step
- perform this stepping movement 24 times per minute for three minutes
- As soon as the three minutes are completed, sit down and count heart rate (carotid or racial pulse) for one full minute to determine rating for your age group.

RATINGS: STEP TEST

RATING (FEMALES)	20-29 (BPM)	30-39 (BPM)	40-49 (BPM)	50-59 (BPM)	>60 (BPM)
6	<85	<88	<91	<94	<97
5	86–95	89–98	92–101	95–104	98–107
4	96–105	99–108	102–111	105–114	108–117
3	106–115	109–118	112–121	115–124	118–127
2	116–125	119–128	122–131	125–134	128–136
1	>126	>128	>132	>135	>137

RATING (MALES)	20-29 (BPM)	30-39 (BPM)	40-49 (BPM)	50-59 (BPM)	>60 (BPM)
6	<80	<83	<86	<89	<92
5	81–90	84–93	87–96	90–99	93–101
4	91–100	94–103	97–106	100–109	102–112
3	101–110	104–113	107–116	110–119	113–122
2	111–120	114–123	117–126	120–129	123–131
1	>121	>124	>127	>130	>132

TWELVE MINUTE RUN, SWIM OR CYCLE TEST

The Twelve Minute Run Test was designed by Dr Kenneth Cooper and made popular in his book 'Aerobics'. He has since added similar tests for swimming and cycling. (These tests can be quite strenuous and you need to know how to pace yourself for them. Consequently, it is advisable that they be done after you have been exercising for 4–6 weeks and not at the very beginning of your program).

Equipment Stop Watch
A level area that is marked out accurately, such as a running track (most high schools have this).

Procedure
- Run (or combine running and walking), swim or cycle for 12 minutes.
- Measure accurately the total distance covered in that time.
- Check with the relevant chart for your fitness category and rating.

RATINGS: TWELVE MINUTE SWIM TEST

RATING (FEMALES)	13–19 (M)	20–29 (M)	30–39 (M)	40–49 (M)	50–59 (M)	>60 (M)
6	>700	>650	>600	>550	>500	>450
5	600–700	550–650	500–600	450–550	400–500	350–450
4	500–600	450–550	400–500	350–450	300–400	250–350
3	425–500	375–450	325–400	275–350	225–300	175–250
2	350–425	300–375	250–325	200–275	150–225	100–175
1	<350	<300	<250	<200	<150	<100

RATINGS: TWELVE MINUTE RUN/WALK TEST

RATING (MALES)	13–19 (KM)	20–29 (KM)	30–39 (KM)	40–49 (KM)	50–59 (KM)	>60 (KM)
6	>3.1	>2.83	>2.71	>2.66	>2.55	>2.51
5	2.8–3.0	2.6–2.8	2.5–2.7	2.5–2.65	2.3–2.54	2.2–2.5
4	2.5–2.7	2.4–2.5	2.3–2.4	2.2–2.4	2.1–2.3	1.9–2.1
3	2.2–2.5	2.1–2.4	2.1–2.3	2.0–2.2	1.9–2.1	1.6–1.9
2	2.1–2.2	2.0–2.1	1.9–2.1	1.8–2.0	1.6–1.9	1.4–1.6
1	<2.1	<1.95	<1.9	<1.8	<1.6	<1.4

RATINGS: TWELVE MINUTE CYCLE TEST

RATING (MALES)	13–19 (KM)	20–29 (KM)	30–39 (KM)	40–49 (KM)	50–59 (KM)	>60 (KM)
6	>9.2	>8.8	>8.4	>8.0	>7.3	>6.4
5	7.7–9.1	7.3–8.7	6.9–8.3	6.5–7.9	5.6–7.2	4.8–6.3
4	6.0–7.6	5.6–7.2	5.2–6.8	4.8–6.4	4.0–5.5	3.6–4.7
3	4.9–5.9	4.5–5.5	4.1–5.2	3.7–4.7	3.3–4.0	3.2–3.6
2	4.4–4.8	4.0–4.4	3.6–4.0	3.2–3.6	2.8–3.2	2.7–3.1
1	<4.4	<4.0	<3.6	<3.2	<2.8	<2.7

RATINGS: TWELVE MINUTE SWIM TEST

RATING (MALES)	13–19 (M)	20–29 (M)	30–39 (M)	40–49 (M)	50–59 (M)	>60 (M)
6	>900	>775	>700	>650	>600	>550
5	775–900	650–775	600–700	550–650	500–600	450–550
4	650–775	550–650	500–600	450–550	400–500	350–450
3	550–650	475–550	425–500	375–450	325–400	275–350
2	450–550	400–475	350–425	300–375	250–325	200–275
1	<450	<400	<350	<300	<250	<200

| RATINGS: TWELVE MINUTE RUN/WALK TEST |||||||
RATING (FEMALES)	13–19 (KM)	20–29 (KM)	30–39 (KM)	40–49 (KM)	50–59 (KM)	>60 (KM)
6	>2.43	>2.34	>2.25	>2.16	>2.10	>1.90
5	2.3–2.4	2.2–2.3	2.1–2.24	2.0–2.1	1.9–2.1	1.8–1.9
4	2.1–2.25	2.0–2.15	1.9–2.05	1.8–1.95	1.7–1.85	1.6–1.75
3	1.9–2.0	1.8–1.95	1.7–1.85	1.6–1.75	1.5–1.65	1.4–1.55
2	1.6–1.85	1.5–1.75	1.5–1.65	1.4–1.55	1.3–1.45	1.25–1.35
1	<1.6	<1.54	<1.52	<1.41	<1.34	<1.25

| RATINGS: TWELVE MINUTE CYCLE TEST |||||||
RATING (FEMALES)	13–19 (KM)	20–29 (KM)	30–39 (KM)	40–49 (KM)	50–59 (KM)	>60 (KM)
6	>7.6	>7.2	>6.8	>6.4	>5.6	>4.8
5	6.1–7.55	5.6–7.15	5.2–6.75	4.8–6.35	4.0–5.55	3.2–4.75
4	4.4–6.0	4.0–5.55	3.6–5.15	3.2–4.75	2.4–3.95	2.0–3.15
3	2.8–4.35	2.4–4.0	2.0–3.55	1.7–3.15	1.2–2.35	1.2–2.0
2	2.1–2.75	1.7–2.35	1.4–1.95	1.1–1.65	1.0–1.15	0.9–1.15
1	<2.0	<1.6	<1.3	<1.2	<0.95	<0.9

ABDOMINAL STRENGTH

Equipment 2.5 weight

Procedure
- Lie on the floor (see figure) so that the angle at the knee is 90°. Feet do not have to be together, but some part of both feet must be in contact with the floor. The feet should not be held or stabilised in any way.
- Place the arms in position for Variation 1. Tilt the pelvis backwards to flatten the lower back onto the floor, then tilt the head forward and smoothly flex the trunk in a controlled manner until Variation 1 is completed. Return to the starting position.
- Repeat steps 2, 3, 4 etc. until unsuccessful. Record the number of the variation of the previous situp (i.e. the last successful situp) as your rating of abdominal strength.
- criteria for unsuccessful situp:
  — lifting either heel off the floor
  — 'throwing' the arms or head forward
  — moving the arms from the nominated position
  — lifting the hips off the floor
  — failing to maintain the 90° knee angle
  — being unable to complete the nominated situp

Variations

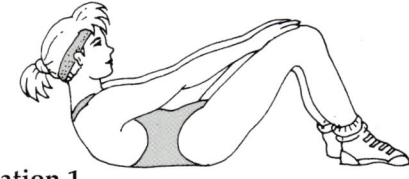

Variation 1
Start: Arms straight, hands resting on top of thighs
Finish: Arms straight, fingertips touching patella

Variation 2
Start: Arms straight, hands resting on top of thighs
Finish: Arms straight, elbows touching patella

Variation 3
Start: Arms across the abdomen, hands gripping the opposite elbows
Finish: Forearms touching the thighs

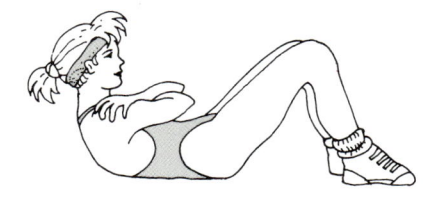

Variation 4
Start: Arms across the chest, hands gripping the opposite shoulders
Finish: Forearms touching the thighs

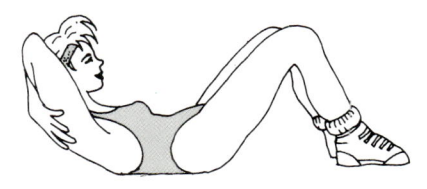

Variation 5
Start: Arms flexed behind the head, hands gripping the opposite shoulders
Finish: Chest touching the thighs

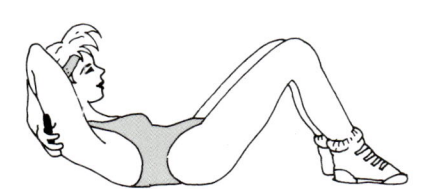

Variation 6
Start: Arms flexed behind the head, hands gripping the opposite sides of a 2.3 kg weight
Finish: Chest touching the thighs

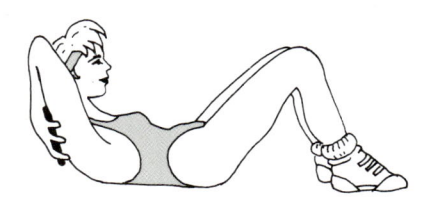

Variation 7
Start: Arms flexed behind the head, hands gripping the opposite sides of a 4.5 kg weight
Finish: Chest touching the thighs

Rating

6	excellent
5	very good
4	good
3	fair
2	poor
1	very poor

Source: Pang P and S M Dortkamp 1987. A new test of abdominal strength.

FLEXIBILITY

The Sit and Reach Test is commonly used to assess flexibility of the muscles of the lower back and the hamstrings at the back of the thigh.

Equipment Sit and Reach Box
(It is possible to improvise with a box and a rule attached to the upper surface. Remember that the score level with the front side of the box is zero)

Procedure
- Sit on the floor with legs and bare feet flat up against the box
- Keep legs straight
- Slowly extend the arms forward, hands together and stretch to touch as far forward along rule as possible
- Hold for 3 seconds
- Read and record distance along rule in centimetres

Rating:

6	20+	Excellent
5	16–20	Very good
4	11–15	Good
3	6–10	Fair
2	0–5	Poor
1	(−6)–0	Very Poor

APPENDIX C

LIST OF INSTITUTIONS WITH SPORTS SCIENCE FACILITIES

Ballarat College of Advanced Education
Sports Performance Unit
PO Box 663
BALLARAT 3350 VIC.
Tel. (03) 30 1800

University of Canberra
Sports Studies Department
PO Box 1
BELCONNEN 2616 ACT
Tel. (062) 62 2284

Catholic College of Education
Dept of Physical Education and Health Sciences
521 Old Northern Road
CASTLE HILL 2154 NSW
Tel. (02) 670 1977

Sports Science and Research Centre
Cumberland College of Health Sciences, University of Sydney
PO Box 170
LIDCOMBE 2141 NSW
Tel. (02) 646 6478

Darling Downs Institute of Advanced Education
PO Darling Heights
TOOWOOMBA 4550 QLD
Tel. (076) 31 2100

Flinders University of South Australia
Sturt Road
BEDFORD PARK 5042 SA
Tel. (08) 275 3911

Footscray Institute of Technology
Human Performance Laboratory
PO Box 64
FOOTSCRAY 3011 VIC
Tel. (03) 689 4069

Phillip Institute of Technology
Sports Performance Unit
Plenty Road
BUNDOORA 3083 VIC
Tel. (03) 468 2200

SPORTEST
Department of Human Movement Studies
University of Queensland
ST LUCIA 4067
Tel. (07) 377 3062

University of NSW
St George Campus
Health and Sports Studies Department
PO Box 88
OATLEY 2223 NSW
Tel. (02) 570 0709

Tasmanian Institute of Technology
PO Box 1214
LAUNCESTON 7250 TAS
Tel. (003) 26 0201

University of Western Australia
Dept. of Human Movements & Rec. Studies
NEDLANDS 6009 WA
Tel. (09) 380 3838

University of Wollongong
Dept. of Human Movement & Sport Science
PO Box 1144
WOLLONGONG 2500 NSW
Tel. (042) 27 0555

AUSTRALIAN SPORTS MEDICINE FEDERATION STATE BRANCHES

New South Wales
PO Box N368
Grosvenor Street
Sydney 2000

Victoria
c/- Phys Ed Dept
PO Box 64
Footscray 3001

Queensland
PO Box 240
St Lucia 4067

South Australia
70 South Terrace
Adelaide 5000

Western Australia
PO Box 57
Claremont 6010

Tasmania
15 Hunter Street
Hobart 7000

Australian Capital Territory
PO Box 191
Civic Square 2608

Northern Territory
PO Box 42133
Casuarina 0811

APPENDIX D

BUYING A PAIR OF RUNNING SHOES

1 The Anatomy of a Shoe

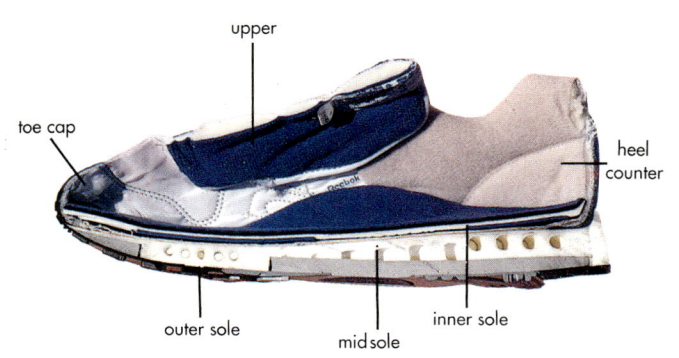

(shoe diagram with labels: upper, toe cap, heel counter, outer sole, mid sole, inner sole)

2 Steps to take and things to consider before going to shop:
(i) look at your old shoes for signs of wear
- heel counter
- uppers
- outsole
- midsole

(ii) Look at yourself
- type of foot – diagram of your footprints helps here
  - normal feet
  - flat feet
  - high-arched feet
- size of feet (length and width)
  - do they differ
- legs — are they
  - knock-kneed
  - bowlegged
- check Q angle?
- body weight

(iii) Have you been injured in the past?
- knees
- heel spurs
- shin splints
- stress fractures
- achilles tendenitis

(iv) Running style
- heel striker
- midfoot or forefoot striker
- pronator/subinator

(v) Where will you run or walk?
- surface – bitumen or grass
- weather – wet/dry

(vi) Go to a store which specialises in running shoes
- take your answers to the questions above
- take along a pair of your running socks and old shoes
- ask for a demo pair
- go in the afternoon – feet swell a little

(vii) Shoe should have 1 cm between longest toe and end of toe box

3 Shoes for other activities may have different requirements:
(I) Walking
- ½ size bigger because of forefoot movement
- flexible forefoot
- straight last without too much inward curve

(ii) Cycling
Needs a firm rather than a flexible sole

(iii) Aerobic Dance
Need to look for
- forefoot cushioning and support
- firm but comfortable leather upper
- firm heel counter for lateral support

APPENDIX E

FURTHER READING

GENERAL

Anderson, R., *Stretching*, Shelter Pub, Bolinas, Calif, 1980.

Australian Fitness and Training, Australian Workout Publications Pty Ltd

Cooper, K., *Aerobics*, Bantam Books Inc., NY, 1968.

Cooper, K., *The New Aerobics*, Bantam Books Inc., NY, 1970.

Cooper, K., *Aerobics for Women*, Bantam Books Inc., NY, 1972.

Corbin, C. & R. Lindsey, *The Ultimate Fitness Book*, Leisure Press. Champaign III, 1984.

Fixx, J. F., *Maximum Sports Performance*, Angus & Robertson, 1985.

Great Quotations, Great Quotations Incorporated, USA.

Getchell, Bud, *Being Fit: a personal guide*, John Wiley & Sons Inc. NY, 1982.

Getchell, Bud, *Physical Fitness: a way of life*, John Wiley & Sons NY, 1979.

Milkin, G., *The Sports Medicine Book*, Little Brown & Co Boston, 1978.

Stewart, G. W., *Every Body's Fitness Book,* 3S Publications, Victoria BC, 1982.

Charkey, B. J., *Physiology of Fitness,* Human Kinetics Pub Inc., Champaign, 1984.

Peterson, Vicky, *Strategies of Champions,* Pan Book, Sydney, London, 1988.

NUTRITION

Athletics Towards 2000, Teachers Resource Materials, 7. *Nutrition for Athletes,* Australian Athletics Union, 1988.

K. & P. Brukner, *Food for Sport,* Heinemann, Aust., 1986.

Katch, F. I. & W. D. McArdle, *Nutrition Weight Control and Exercise,* Lea & Febider, Pa, 1983.

Saxeby, C., *Nutrition for Life,* 1988.

Stanton, R., *Food for Health,* WB Saunders, Sydney, 1979.

Jonas, S. & P. Rodetsky, *Pace Walking — The Balanced Way to Aerobic Health,* Cram Pub, NY.

WALKING

The Walking Magazine U.S.A.

Kash, A. & J. Rippe, *Fitness Walking For Women,* Putnam Pub Group, NY.

RUNNING

Australian Runner, editor/publisher Terry O'Halloran.

de Castella, R., *On Running,* Currey O'Neil, Melbourne, 1984.

Fixx, J., *The Complete Book of Running,* Random House Inc., NY, 1977.

Ullyot, J., *Running Free: A guide for women runners and their friends,* G.P. Putman's Sons. NY, 1980.

SWIMMING

Magischo, E W. & C., Ferguson Brennan, *Swim for the Health of it,* Payfield Pub. Co., Palo Alto, 1985.

CYCLING

Bicycle Guide, Raben/Bicycle Guide Partners, Boston, USA.

Free Wheeling

AEROBIC DANCE

Main, S., G.W. Stewart & R. Bradshaw, *Fit All Over,* 3-S Fitness Group, Victoria, BC, 1984.

WEIGHT TRAINING

Cook, B. & B. W. Stewart, *Get Strong,* 3-S Fitness Group, Victoria, BC, 1981.

Kirkley, G. & Goodbody, *The Manual of Weight-training,* Stanley Paul, London, 1986.

Reynolds, Bill, *Weight Training for Beginners,* Contemporary Books Inc. Chicago, 1982.

Weider, B. & R. Kennedy, *Pumping Up,* Sterling Pub. Co. NY, 1985

CROSS TRAINING/TRIATHLON

Horning, D., *Triathlon Lifestyle of Fitness,* Pocket Books, NY, 1985.

Tinley, S., *Winning Triathlon,* Contemporary Books, Chicago, 1986.

ACKNOWLEDGMENTS

Very special thanks are due to Margaret Barrett and Enid Ginn for their vital contributions to the book, to Marion Stell for her valuable input and to Peter Bethune, designer and manufacturer of Aussie Fit Water Weights, for his input on dehydration.

Thanks also to Pam Brewster, Claire Craig, Leonie Bremer-Kamp, Karen Ball, Liz Seymour, David Smith and Rosemary Craig, from Collins/Angus & Robertson; and to the Sheraton Mirage Gold Coast, who provided the locations for many of the photographs.

A special thank you to my family and friends who modelled for the photographs, and to Renee Chambellant, who was in charge of make-up.

PHOTOGRAPHIC CREDITS

Cover and title page: Ian Golding. Make-up: Madonna Melrose. Contents page (top right and bottom); Pages 12-13, 49, 62-63, 72-73, 84(top left), 86(top right), 108, Don Miskell. Pages 16-17, 24-25, Scott Cameron. A special thank you to Ian Golding for the remaining photographs. He is a pleasure to work with.

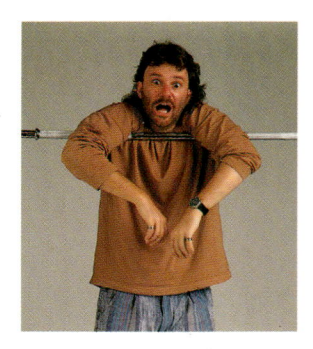

Ian Golding